Apple Pro Training Series

Xsan Quick-Reference Guide, Second Edition

Adam Green and Matthew Geller

Apple Pro Training Series: Xsan Quick-Reference Guide, Second Edition

Adam Green and Matthew Geller

Copyright © 2006 Apple Computer, Inc.

Published by Peachpit Press. For information on Peachpit Press books, contact:
Peachpit Press
1249 Eighth Street
Berkeley, CA 94710
(510) 524-2178
(800) 283-9444
Fax: (510) 524-2221
http://www.peachpit.com

To report errors, please send a note to errata@peachpit.com

Peachpit Press is a division of Pearson Education

ISBN 0-321-43232-0

9 8 7 6 5 4 3 2

Printed and bound in the United States of America

Table of Contents

Table of Contents

Lesson 5

Lesson 6

Lesson 7

Lesson 8

Lesson 9

Lesson 10

Lesson 11

About the Authors

Adam Green has been involved in the post-production and music industries since the mid 80's. With a start as a recording engineer, he worked for Avid/Digidesign, helping major post-production and music studios convert to their new technology. He has also worked as an editor, camera operator, and location sound mixer for television and film. He has taught Avid and Final Cut Pro classes at such training facilities as Video Symphony and Moviola, and was the first trainer for Apple Computer's Final Cut Pro certification. He is currently Apple's Senior Manager of Pro Applications and Market Development for Latin America.

Matthew Geller is the co-founder of Meta Media Creative Technologies, a Chicago-based firm that helps creative facilities leverage technology to its fullest potential. He is a senior trainer for Apple's Pro Applications Division, assisting in their courseware development and leading train-the-trainer classes. He has authored chapters in numerous books for Peachpit Press, including Optimizing Your Final Cut Pro System and DVD Studio Pro 4. He teaches master classes at facilities as diverse as World Wrestling Entertainment and the BBC. To learn more, go to http://metamediatech.com.

1

Xsan Overview

Xsan is a storage area network file system (ACFS, or Apple Cluster File System) and a management application (Xsan Admin) you can use to provide expandable storage to users or applications on client computers with shared high-speed access.

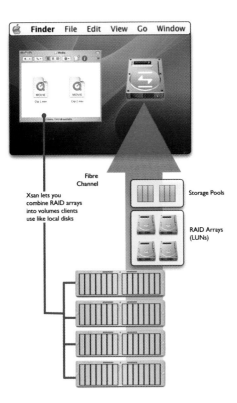

The Network

A storage area network (SAN) is a way of connecting computers to storage devices that gives users very fast access to files and gives administrators the ability to expand storage capacity as needed without interrupting users.

An Xsan SAN consists of the following:

- Volumes of shared storage, stored on Apple Xserve RAID (Redundant Array of Independent Disks) systems, available to clients as mounted volumes that they can use like local disks

- At least one computer acting as a metadata controller that coordinates access to the shared volumes

- Client computers that access storage in accordance with established permissions and quotas

- Underlying Fibre Channel and Ethernet networks

The following illustration shows the physical components of a typical Xsan SAN:

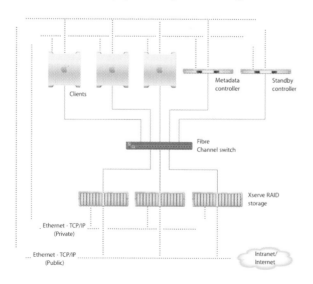

SAN Volumes

Shared SAN volumes that you create in the Xsan Admin application will appear to the client as a single local volume. You can create these volumes by selecting a combination of RAID arrays to be included in a pool, which, in turn, is added to create the volume. Volumes can be up to 1024 terabytes (TB) in size, which means a client machine will be able to display up to eight 1024 TB volumes on its desktop. Furthermore, clients can write one file that is 1024 TB in size, or create up to 4 billion files and directories per volume!

Metadata Controllers

You must assign at least one computer to become a controller when setting up your SAN. This machine has the job of maintaining the volume metadata of the SAN, file journaling, and concurrent access to files. This controller "remembers" which RAIDs are part of a pool, and how you have configured your pools to make volumes. Although the controller is in charge of these tasks, the actual data is stored on the SAN. In the event of failure of the main controller, Xsan will automatically switch to the backup controller. The backup controller is aware of how the SAN is configured, so if failure occurs, and the backup kicks into action, clients are often unaware that anything has happened.

Clients

Machines that have access to the SAN are called clients. You can have a total of 64 clients in Xsan with concurrent block-level access to a shared volume. Clients are configured in the Xsan Admin application and are able to mount the shared storage if given access. The files the client reads and writes are sent via the Fibre Channel connection, but other client/controller communication is made possible by an Ethernet "out-of-band" network. An unlimited number of clients may indirectly access data from the SAN if any client is configured to host a network service such as file sharing (AFP, SMB/CIFS, and NFS).

2 Hardware and Software Requirements

There are a number of components necessary to configure a SAN:

- Apple Xsan software

- Supported controller and client computers

- Supported storage devices

- Fibre Channel fabric, adapters, and switches

- Ethernet network

- Directory services (optional)

- Outgoing mail service (optional)

Supported Computers

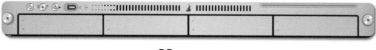

Xserve

Xserve G5

Xserve G5 Cluster Node

Power Mac G5

**Power Mac G4
Dual 800MHz or faster**

Memory

Metadata Controllers

Controllers should have a minimum of 512 MB of RAM. In cases where you will have more than one volume, allocate 512 MB RAM per volume for optimal performance. ECC (Error Correction Code) memory is preferred for RAM in metadata controllers.

Client Machines

Client machines should have a minimum of 256 MB of RAM, with 512 MB of RAM recommended. If you are running any of the professional applications (Final Cut Pro, Shake, Motion, DVD Studio Pro, Logic, Soundtrack Pro, or Aperture), the recommended system requirements will vary between 384 MB and up to 4 GB of RAM.

Supported Operating Systems

- Max OS X v.10.3.9 (Xsan 1.2 for Mac OS X v10.3)

- Mac OS X v10.4 or later (Xsan 1.2 for Mac OS X v10.4)

- Mac OS Server v10.3.9 (Xsan 1.2 for Mac OS X v10.3)

- Mac OS Server v10.4 or later (Xsan 1.2 for Mac OS X v10.4)

Version Compatibility

Controller	Client	Compatible?
Xsan 1.0.x or 1.2 (Mac OS X v10.3)	Xsan 1.0.x or 1.2 (Mac OS X v10.3)	Yes
	Xsan 1.2 (Mac OS X v10.4)	No
	StorNext 2.4	Yes
	StorNext 2.5	No
Xsan 1.2 (Mac OS X v10.4)	Xsan 1.0.x or 1.2 (Mac OS X v10.3)	Yes
	Xsan 1.2 (Mac OS X v10.4)	Yes
	StorNext 2.4	No
	StorNext 2.5	Yes
StorNext 2.4	Xsan 1.0.x or 1.2 (Mac OS X v10.3)	Yes
	Xsan 1.2 (Mac OS X v10.4)	No
	StorNext 2.4	Yes
	StorNext 2.5	No
StorNext 2.5	Xsan 1.0.x or 1.2 (Mac OS X v10.3)	Yes
	Xsan 1.2 (Mac OS X v10.4)	Yes
	StorNext 2.4	Yes
	StorNext 2.5	Yes

Important: Whether you are running Panther or Tiger systems, your metadata controllers (MDCs) must always have software versions (both Xsan and Mac OS) that are equal to or more recent than the most recent client versions. Specifically, if any client in your Xsan network is running Xsan 1.2 on Mac OS X 10.4.3 or later, then your MDCs must also be updated to Xsan 1.2 on Mac OS X 10.4.3 or later.

Using ADIC's StorNext software version 2.4 or later, you will also be able to integrate Xsan with the following operating systems:

- **Windows** (Microsoft)

- **AIX** (IBM)

- **IRIX** (SGI)

- **Solaris** (Sun)

- **Linux**

For more information on StorNext software, go to www.adic.com.

Storage Devices

Use Xserve RAID systems for optimum compatibility with Xsan. This book assumes you are using Xserve RAID systems for your storage devices.

Apple Xserve RAID consists of two controllers, each holding up to seven Apple Drive Modules. Each controller should have the maximum 512 MB of RAM installed for optimal performance with Xsan.

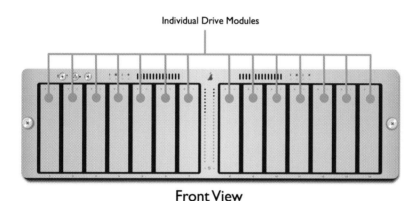

Individual Drive Modules

Front View

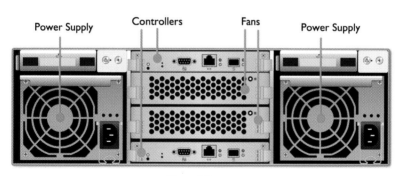

Power Supply   Controllers   Fans   Power Supply

Rear View

Fibre Channel Fabric

In order to attain high data transfer rates (uncompressed high-definition video, for example), a Fibre Channel network is implemented to connect clients, controllers, and storage to your SAN. This will be the main data connection for large files you will transfer throughout your SAN.

A number of components make up the Fibre Channel fabric, including copper or optical cabling, small form factor pluggables (SFPs), host bus adapters (HBAs), and supported Fibre Channel switches.

Fibre Channel PCI Express and PCI-X HBA Cards

Xsan supports Apple Fibre Channel PCI Express, PCI-X, and PCI cards to act as the host bus adapter in both your server and client nodes.

Apple's Fibre Channel HBA cards have two connections on the back where you connect the card to your Fibre Channel cables.

Apple Fibre Channel PCI Express Card

Fibre Channel Switches

Much like Ethernet switches, Fibre Channel switches must be used to connect all of your clients, controllers, and storage together. There are many types of Fibre Channel switches, and Apple has tested and approved a few of them for use with Xsan:

- Brocade SilkWorm 3200, 3250, 3800, 3850, 3900, and 12000 series

- QLogic SANbox 2-8, SANbox 2-16, SANbox 2-64, SANbox 5200, and SANbox 5202

- Emulex SAN Switch 355, 375, and 9200

- Cisco MDS 9120, 9140, 9216, 9506, and 9509

Each of these switches must be configured as open fabric, where each port sees every other port. In general, the default configuration of these switches will work with Xsan. If you need to reconfigure or verify the switch settings, you need to connect to the switch with your Macintosh via an Ethernet connection. From there, you can run either a standard browser to view the switch configuration or specialized Java applications built specifically for switch setup.

See Lesson 7 for more information on switch setup.

Metadata Network

Regardless of the size of your SAN implementation, you will also need another out-of-band network, which means that although the clients are connected to the rest of the SAN through Fibre Channel connections, the metadata and file access communication travel on a separate Ethernet network. Splitting the connection into two independent networks ensures that no "non-metadata" data packets clog up the Fibre Channel network, giving you the maximum bandwidth for large data files.

Needless to say, both a Fibre Channel switch and an Ethernet switch (1000 Base-T recommended, also known as Gigabit Ethernet) are necessary to configure Xsan. It is also desirable to keep the "chatter" separate from the out-of-band network by connecting clients to the Internet using a secondary Ethernet port. If your computer has only one Ethernet port and you want access to a network outside your SAN, you can place an additional Ethernet PCI card in your client computers.

3

Xsan Topologies

There are numerous ways for you to implement your new SAN. The following three examples show typical topologies for production environments. Again, these are guides, intended to provide a summary of the previously discussed information as you plan and acquire your equipment for integration.

Topology Example 1

In this example, we are using the most basic of topologies. We have a total of 3.9 TB of storage utilizing a fully populated RAID (5.6 TB model). The SAN's bandwidth availability with one fully populated Xserve RAID is 160 to 200 megabytes per second (MB/s). This SAN is isolated; that is, the system is not connected to an outer network. This is perfect for implementations in which highly confidential content is being edited. Also, we are not utilizing a centralized directory, so clients will be locally authenticated (the server will not be in control of the login process), and the "chatter" on the metadata network will be kept to a minimum. In order to access and set up either the Fibre Channel switch or the Xserve RAID, an additional connection must be made from a separate computer outside the network.

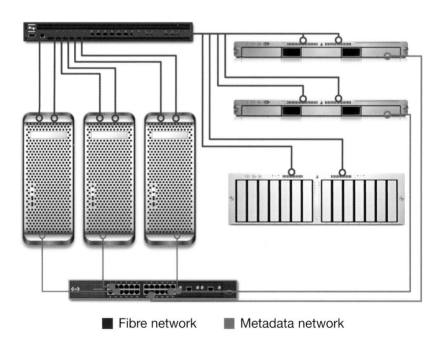

■ Fibre network   ■ Metadata network

Storage

- 1 x Xserve RAID 5.6 TB (fully populated with 400 GB drive modules)
- 512 MB cache per controller (1 GB total)

Fibre Channel Switch

- 1 x Apple qualified Fibre Channel switch

Metadata Controllers

- Xserve, Xserve G5, or Xserve G5 cluster node
- 1 GB RAM per controller
- Apple Fibre Channel PCI-X card
- Mac OS X Server v10.3.6 or later
- Apple Xsan software
- PCI video card (optional)

Metadata Network

- 1 x unmanaged gigabit Ethernet switch

Client Workstations

- Power Macintosh G5 or Power Macintosh G4 Dual 800 or faster
- Apple Fibre Channel PCI Express or PCI-X card
- Mac OS X v10.3.6 or later
- Apple Xsan software

Topology Example 2

In this larger implementation, we have six clients accessing a total of 7.28 TB of storage. The SAN's bandwidth availability is roughly 320 to 400 MB/s. This SAN is connected to an outer network, shown in green. Notice that all trivial Ethernet components are routed to this outer network, and only the nodes of the SAN are on the metadata network. Further, we have a standby metadata controller available to take over MDC duties if the primary MDC fails. For directory services, we have three choices:

- The primary MDC is the open directory master of the SAN, with the standby MDC as a replica.

- The standby MDC is the open directory master of the SAN, with the primary MDC as the replica.

- The directory has been moved to the outer network, thereby allowing the Xserve units to just be MDCs (recommended).

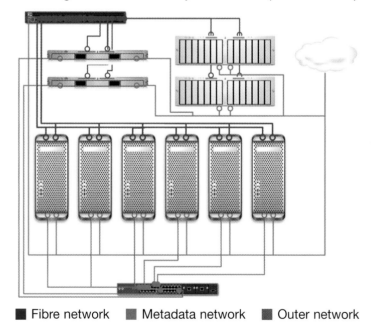

■ Fibre network   ■ Metadata network   ■ Outer network

Storage

- 2 x Xserve RAID 5.6 TB (populated with six 400 GB drive modules per controller; the seventh is a hot spare, not used in the storage calculation)
- 512 MB cache per controller (1 GB total)

Fibre Channel Switch

- 1 x Apple qualified Fibre Channel switch

Metadata Controllers

- Xserve, Xserve G5, or Xserve G5 cluster node
- 1 GB RAM per controller
- Apple Fibre Channel PCI-X card
- Mac OS X Server v10.3.6 or later
- Apple Xsan software
- PCI video card (optional)

Metadata Network

- 1 x unmanaged gigabit Ethernet switch

Client Workstations

- Power Macintosh G5 or Power Macintosh G4 Dual 800 or faster
- Apple Fibre Channel PCI-X card
- Apple Ethernet PCI-X card
- Mac OS X v10.3.6 or later
- Apple Xsan software

Outer Network

Mac OS X Server running Open Directory to provide directory services, or a system running a similar service such as Microsoft Active Directory.

Topology Example 3

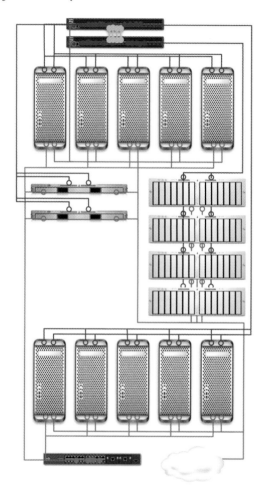

■ Fibre network ■ Metadata network ■ Outer network

In this topology, ten clients share 16 TB of storage. The SAN's bandwidth availability with four semi-populated Xserve RAIDs is a whopping 640 to 800 MB/s. Because of the number of Fibre cables in this topology (32 total), an additional switch has been implemented. Data cascades effortlessly between the two switches because a high-bandwidth interswitch link (ISL) has been made with six user ports on each switch. Think of it as a data river that flows bidirectionally between each switch. A primary and a standby MDC are mandatory with such a large implementation. To keep their roles simple and efficient, the directory is implemented on the outer network.

Storage

- 4 x Xserve RAID 7 TB (populated with six 500 GB drive modules per controller; the seventh is a hot spare, not used in the storage calculation)
- 512 MB cache per controller (1 GB total)

Fibre Channel Switch

- 2 x Apple qualified Fibre Channel switch

Metadata Controllers

- Xserve, Xserve G5, or Xserve G5 cluster node
- 1 GB RAM per controller
- Apple Fibre Channel PCI-X card
- Mac OS X Server v10.3.6 or later
- Apple Xsan software
- PCI video card (optional)

Ethernet Switch (Metadata Network)

- 1 x unmanaged Ethernet gigabit switch

Client Workstations

- Power Macintosh G5 or Power Macintosh G4 Dual 800 or faster
- Apple Fibre Channel PCI Express or PCI-X card
- Apple Ethernet PCI-X card
- Mac OS X v10.3.6 or later
- Apple Xsan software

Outer Network

Mac OS X Server running Open Directory to provide directory services, or a system running a similar service such as Active Directory.

4

Setting Up Your Storage

The Apple Xserve RAID (redundant array of independent disks) is a group of hard drives that appears to the host Power Mac as a single high-speed storage unit. RAID systems enable you to increase storage capacity and get the performance, reliability, and data protection needed for video production, which is not possible from a single hard drive. RAID drives inside the array operate simultaneously, increasing overall throughput. Some or all of the following techniques are used in RAID technology:

- RAID level 0: Striping data across multiple drives for storage performance
- RAID level 1: Mirroring for redundancy
- RAID level 3 and 5: Parity for data protection (plus others)

Most RAID configurations combine these techniques to provide a balance of protection and performance. Striping divides a logical drive into data blocks, or stripes, that are distributed across an array of physical drives. Striping a set of disks improves storage performance because each drive operates concurrently. However, striping alone, known as RAID level 0, offers no data protection. Mirroring involves writing identical copies of all data to a pair of physical drives. This results in very high data reliability; if one drive fails, the data is still available on the remaining drive. However, it also results in a storage efficiency of only 50 percent, because two physical drives are required to achieve a single drive's capacity. Mirroring alone is known as RAID level 1. Parity provides data protection without requiring a complete duplication of the drive contents. In the event of drive failure, parity information can be used with data on the surviving drives to reconstruct the contents of a failed drive. Parity data can be stored on a dedicated drive, as in RAID 3, or distributed across an array of drives, as in RAID 5. Parity provides much greater storage efficiency than mirroring—up to 85 percent for a set of seven drives.

Calculating the Bandwidth Need

Xsan throughput lets you work well within the bandwidth requirements for most common video formats.

This table shows examples of the average bandwidth used for various video formats. They will vary slightly depending on which card or device is used for capture. Also bear in mind that these numbers reflect a per-stream value.

Bandwidth Requirements

Standard Definition	Bandwidth per Stream
MiniDV, DVCAM, DVCPRO	3.6 MB/s
DVCPRO 50	7.1 MB/s
Uncompressed SD (8-bit) 30/25 fps	20 MB/s
Uncompressed SD (10-bit) 30/25 fps	27 MB/s
Compressed High Definition	
HDV	3.6 MB/s
DVCPRO HD	5.7 MB/s to 14 MB/s
Uncompressed High Definition	
720p 24fps (8-bit)	42 MB/s
720p 24fps (10-bit)	56 MB/s
720p 60fps (8-bit)	104 MB/s
1080p 24fps (8-bit)	93 MB/s
1080i 30fps (8-bit)	116 MB/s
1080p 24fps (10-bit)	124 MB/s
1080i 30fps (10-bit)	155 MB/s

Bandwidth need is based upon the following:

1. The number of clients you will have on the SAN

2. The highest level of video, film, or audio formats your facility uses

3. The maximum number of real-time streams you require to work on recurring projects

To calculate bandwidth need, simply multiply these three considerations. This yields a value, in megabytes per second (MB/s) that determines the theoretical maximum need at any given moment.

Two examples will illustrate the calculation:

- A 10-seat SAN for a news facility works entirely with package editing using the DV25 format. Each editor uses primarily an A/B roll technique, as well as multiple images onscreen simultaneously, and therefore needs up to three streams of real-time availability.

  So this SAN's bandwidth need is
  10 clients x 3 streams x 3.6 MB/s= 108 MB/s

- A three-seat boutique post facility SAN uses SD most days, but is flirting with doing high-end 720p 24-frame-based work in 10-bit uncompressed as well. We'll give them a luxurious three streams of real time in this format, provided that they have the top-of-the-line G5s to do it.

  So this SAN's bandwidth need is
  3 clients x 3 streams x 56 MB/s= 504 MB/s

Calculating the Bandwidth Availability

Bandwidth availability is based on the following:

- Number of LUNs (logical unit numbers)
- Number of physical disks per LUN
- RAID level of the LUNs
- How the LUNs are gathered into storage pools
- The nature and redundancy of the Fibre network

As a rule of thumb, consider that a single Xserve RAID controller, after file system overhead, can transfer roughly 80 to 100 MB of user data per second (160 to 200 MB per Xserve RAID system). If your SAN must support an application running on multiple clients that requires specific throughput on each client, you can use this number to estimate the number of Xserve RAID systems necessary to support the aggregate transfer rate.

This formula will generally aggregate upward to the current maximum size of an Xsan volume, which is 1024 TB. This means, for example, that four Xserve RAIDs, with eight seven-drive LUNs, combined into a single storage pool, are currently yielding a total bandwidth availability of 640 to 800 MB/s.

Metadata Storage Requirements

To estimate the amount of space required for Xsan volume metadata, assume that 10 million files on a volume will require roughly 10 GB of metadata on the volume's metadata storage pool.

Raid Levels for Video Work with Xsan

For video media work, there is little reason for going with any RAID level other than RAID 5 when using Xserve RAIDs for media storage, since the built-in RAID 5 optimization makes their performance very close to RAID 0. Xserve RAIDs out of the box come preconfigured for RAID 5. Render volumes could arguably be RAID level 0—there is no need for backup because in a failed situation renders can easily be recreated. Raid level 1 is an option for your metadata and journaling pool since the minimum number of drives necessary is two, and you will have true redundancy in a mirroring situation.

Minimum Number of Drives per LUN

RAID 0	2
RAID 1	2
RAID 3	3
RAID 5	3

Striping Definitions

RAID 0 offers the best performance but provides no data protection. If one hard drive fails, all data is lost. RAID 0 distributes data evenly across a stripe on the selected drives.

Select two or more drives to use this RAID level.

RAID 1 offers the best data protection but the least efficient storage capacity. All but one of the selected hard drives can fail without data loss.

Select two or more drives to use this RAID level.

RAID 3

RAID 3 offers performance and data protection. One hard drive can fail without data loss. RAID 3 distributes data across a stripe on the selected drives except one drive which is used for parity information.

Select three or more drives to use this RAID level.

RAID 5

RAID 5 offers the best mix of performance and data protection. One hard drive can fail without data loss. RAID 5 distributes parity information across a stripe on the selected drives.

Select three or more drives to use this RAID level.

RAID 0 + 1

RAID 0 + 1 is a hybrid offering performance and data protection but less efficient storage capacity. One hard drive can fail without data loss. RAID 0 + 1 stripes data across mirrored pairs of the selected drives.

Select four or six drives to use this RAID level.

LUNs, Storage Pools, and Volumes

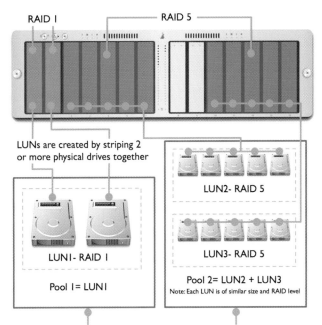

RAID 1 — RAID 5

LUNs are created by striping 2 or more physical drives together

LUN2- RAID 5

LUN1- RAID 1

LUN3- RAID 5

Pool 1= LUN1

Pool 2= LUN2 + LUN3

Note: Each LUN is of similar size and RAID level

Storage pools are created by adding 1 or more LUNs together. Data is then striped across all LUNs in a pool for maximum bandwidth

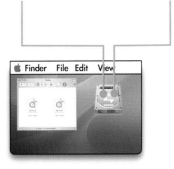

 Finder   File   Edit   View

1 or more storage pools make up the volume that a client sees on the desktop

Striping or Slicing

Normally, LUNs are created by striping or mirroring the entire contents of a physical drive module, which means that as you fill up your drives, the bandwidth decreases. This is because the area toward the inner part of the drive is slower in reads and writes than the outer portion of the drive. Slicing allows you to create arrays with similar speed characteristics. You can divide a LUN into as many as six slices. Each slice pairs the portions of the drive with the same portions on its other paired drives. Xsan will recognize these slices as individual LUNs, starting from the first slice (the outer, or fastest, part of the drive) to the last (the inner, or slowest part).

Striping

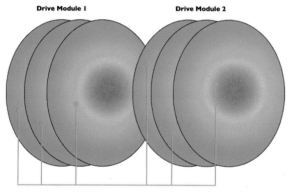

LUN1- All areas of drive strip together, slow and fast

Slicing

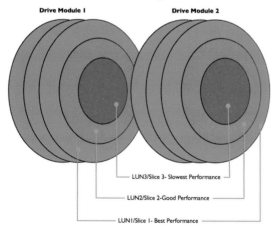

LUN3/Slice 3- Slowest Performance

LUN2/Slice 2-Good Performance

LUN1/Slice 1- Best Performance

Xserve RAID Striping Examples

There are numerous ways to stripe your available Xserve RAID units, depending on the number of RAIDs, as well as your bandwidth need, requirements for audio and render space, as well as other factors such as AFP/NFS/SMB file sharing LUNs.

The following sections present a few examples of how you may divide up your available RAIDs for use with Xsan. Because this will be one of the more creative tasks in the Xsan configuration, we will coin this term *LUNscaping*.

In all implementations of Xsan, it is highly recommended that you create a separate metadata and journaling pool that resides on its own controller of your Xserve RAID. This will allow the controller to be optimized for dealing with these small metadata files and give you the best possible bandwidth out of your SAN. If you are not able to dedicate one controller for this task, then it is possible to share the metadata and journaling controller with other data pools. Realize, however, that if you decide to mix the metadata and journaling information with regular data, you will not be able to expand the volume in the future.

One Xserve RAID

Option 1

This configuration assumes that the media pool contains both metadata and journaling, as well as user data. This method can be used when you need to get the greatest bandwidth from your small SAN, and the number of users is minimal.

This configuration will yield approximately 160 to 200 MB/s and can be used for DV and SD capture and playback.

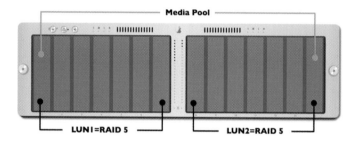

Option 2

In this setup, we have created a LUN specifically for metadata and journaling information. If assigned properly in Xsan Admin, this pool will not be able to be used for any other type of media. It has been created as a RAID level 1, which means that either drive could fail, and the other drive would take over its duties.

The media pool comprises two LUNs, each RAID 5. This configuration will still yield approximately 160 to 200 MB/s bandwidth, so it is suitable for DV and SD recording and playback.

There is also an additional render pool composed of a two-drive RAID 0. Although we recommend placing render media on local hard drives, this is a viable alternative if the render media must reside on the SAN. It is striped as RAID 0 for speed, which means we have no redundancy in case of a drive malfunction. This is not an issue, however, since render files can easily be recreated in case of a drive failure.

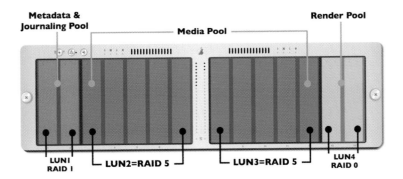

Two Xserve RAIDs

Option 1

When configuring two or more RAIDs, it is optimal to have a separate metadata and journaling pool. The render pool has been striped as RAID level 5 for redundancy, and the audio pool is striped as a mirrored RAID level 1. The rest of the drives are all incorporated in one large video pool and should yield approximately 240 to 300 MB/s throughput.

This configuration is suitable for multiple users recording and playing back DV, SD, and HD material.

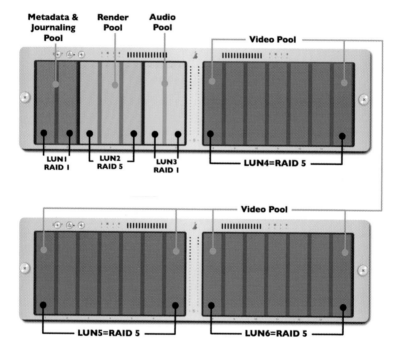

Option 2

Similar to option 1, this configuration could be utilized when the bandwidth need is not as great, and the quantity of render files will be much more substantial.

We have also increased our capacity for audio files because its pool has increased in size as well.

This configuration will yield approximately 160 to 200 MB/s when writing to the video pool, and it is optimized for DV and SD material.

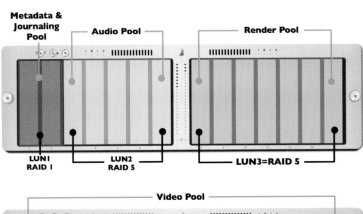

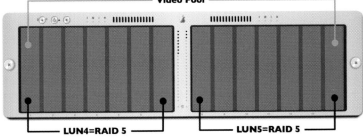

Three Xserve RAIDs

Option 1

Identical to the previous example, this option simply adds another Xserve RAID to our video pool. This addition increases our available bandwidth by 160 MB/s, giving us a total of 320 to 400 MB/s from our video pool.

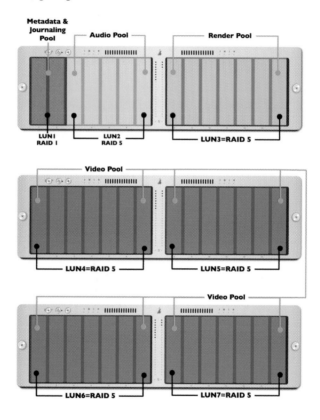

Option 2

This configuration takes into account that for optimum performance, the metadata and journaling pool should occupy its own controller. Notice that we have placed one hot spare in case of a drive failure, but left the remaining drive slots empty in the first controller. This configuration will yield approximately 400 to 500 MB/s when writing to the video pool, and is optimized for DV, SD, and some HD material.

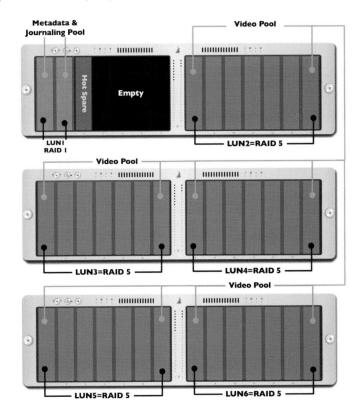

Four Xserve RAIDs

Option 1

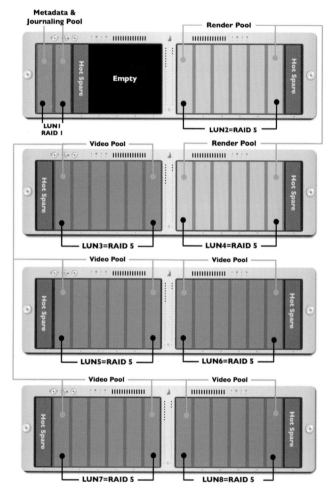

Option 2

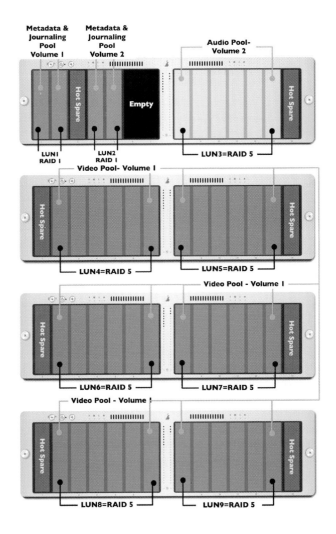

Xserve RAID Slicing Examples

Xsan supports LUN sizes of 2 TB or smaller. However, if you're using an Xserve RAID that provides LUNs larger than 2 TB (such as Xserve RAID installations that use 500 GB hard drives), you can use RAID Admin to create RAID sets that are smaller than 2 TB by using a feature known as slicing.

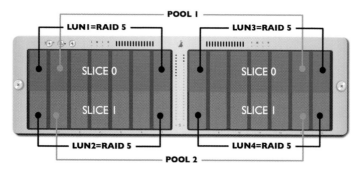

In the diagram, the 3.5 TB LUN that comprises the drives on the left side of the Xserve RAID (controlled by the upper controller) has been sliced into two LUNs (LUN1, LUN2); the 3.5 TB LUN that comprises the drives on the right side of the Xserve RAID (controlled by the lower controller) has also been sliced into two LUNs (LUN3, LUN4). It is recommended to slice the available storage into as few slices as possible.

When creating pools in Xsan Admin, you would create two pools in this example.

- Pool 1: LUN1 + LUN3. These slices have a LUN ID of 0, or slice 0. These outer slices are slightly faster than the inner slices, so this pool is faster than pool 2.

- Pool 2: LUN2 + LUN4. These slices have a LUN ID of 1, or slice 1. This pool is slightly slower than pool 1.

In this example, assume that the metadata and journaling pool is located on a separate Xserve RAID.

Choose Fill as the Allocation Strategy for the Volume when using the slicing method.

For tips on correlating LUNs to RAID slices, please refer to Lesson 8.

Raid Admin Utility

Raid Admin utility lets you set up and configure your Xserve RAID units. Install the application from the provided CD, or download the latest version from www.apple.com. Once it is installed, you will be able to connect to your RAID via an Ethernet connection. Each controller on the RAID has one Ethernet port. It is necessary to connect to only one of the controllers in order to configure and set up your RAID.

Ethernet Connection- Controller 1

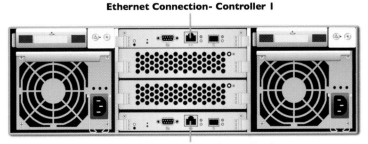

Ethernet Connection- Controller 2

When you first take your Xserve RAID out of the box and plug it in, you will notice that the front drive lights are flashing, which means that the drives are creating the data set, and this might take some time. With a fully populated 7 TB RAID, the dataset creation will take approximately 40 hours. Each time you create a RAID set, expect the drives to take some time to do their stuff. The good news: A background formatting option allows you to use the RAID set almost immediately after the initialization has started. Until RAID sets are completely built, however, there will be a slight decrease in read performance.

RAID Admin Client Connection

Out of the box, your Xserve RAID is set to communicate using Bonjour. This means that the RAID can broadcast its IP to any other client on its subnet. Change the network preferences of the computer running RAID Admin in order to connect to your RAID.

On your client computer, open System Preferences and choose DHCP for your Ethernet connection.

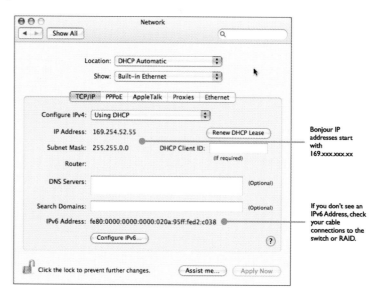

RAID Admin Application

Adding Your RAID

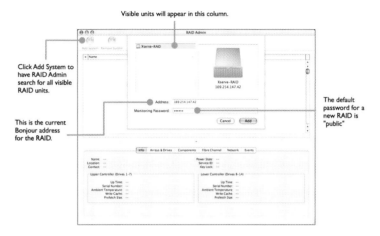

Visible units will appear in this column.

Click Add System to have RAID Admin search for all visible RAID units.

This is the current Bonjour address for the RAID.

The default password for a new RAID is "public"

Raid Monitoring and Information

After connecting to the RAID, you will be able to monitor its drive status, power, fibre channel connectivity, and ethernet connections. This RAID is showing a red light for the fibre channel connection which means the RAID is currently not connected to a fibre channel switch or HBA.

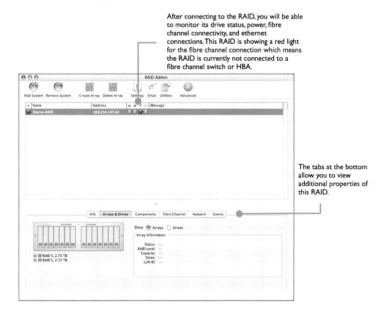

The tabs at the bottom allow you to view additional properties of this RAID.

Viewing Arrays and Drives

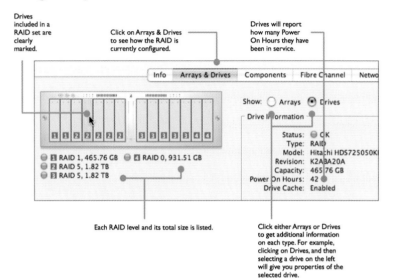

Drives included in a RAID set are clearly marked.

Click on Arrays & Drives to see how the RAID is currently configured.

Drives will report how many Power On Hours they have been in service.

Each RAID level and its total size is listed.

Click either Arrays or Drives to get additional information on each type. For example, clicking on Drives, and then selecting a drive on the left will give you properties of the selected drive.

Viewing Components

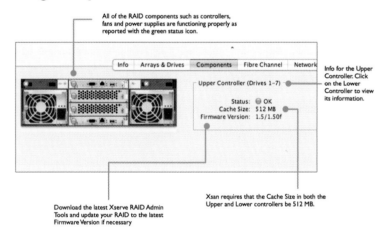

All of the RAID components such as controllers, fans and power supplies are functioning properly as reported with the green status icon.

Info for the Upper Controller. Click on the Lower Controller to view its information.

Download the latest Xserve RAID Admin Tools and update your RAID to the latest Firmware Version if necessary

Xsan requires that the Cache Size in both the Upper and Lower controllers be 512 MB.

Deleting an Array

Since Xserve RAIDs come preconfigured as RAID level 5, you must first delete the current arrays if you want to change the default setup.

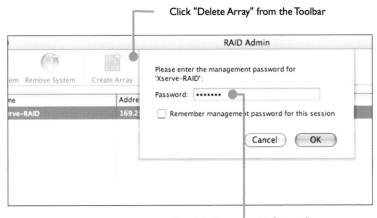

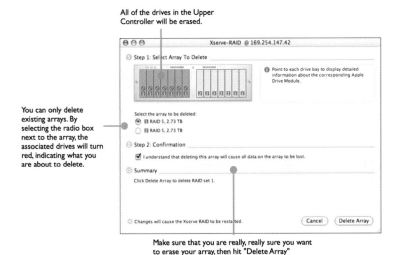

Creating an Array

Click "Create Array" from the Toolbar

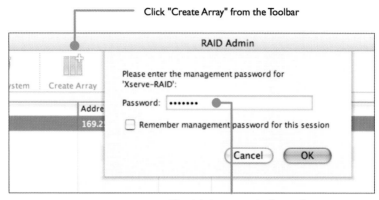

The default password is "private"

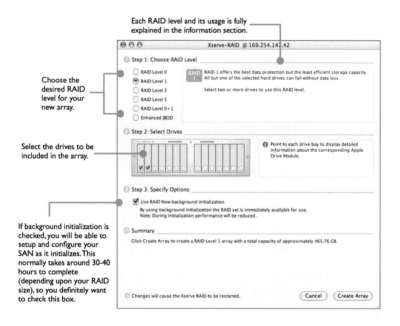

Each RAID level and its usage is fully explained in the information section.

Choose the desired RAID level for your new array.

Select the drives to be included in the array.

If background initialization is checked, you will be able to setup and configure your SAN as it initializes. This normally takes around 30-40 hours to complete (depending upon your RAID size), so you definitely want to check this box.

Xserve RAID Performance Settings

In RAID Admin Settings, take a moment to check the Performance tab and select the following settings for maximum performance in Xsan. These settings should be confirmed every time the Xserve RAID is powered up or restarted.

Enable both controller and individual drive caches.

Steady Streaming Mode should be unchecked to allow the controller to run at maximum throughput.

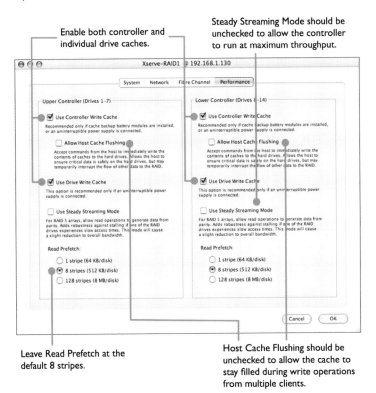

Leave Read Prefetch at the default 8 stripes.

Host Cache Flushing should be unchecked to allow the cache to stay filled during write operations from multiple clients.

Setting Up Your Metadata Controller

In this chapter, we assume that you are setting up a metadata controller using a supported Apple Macintosh computer. This controller can be running either of the following:

- Mac OS X version 10.3.6 or later
- Mac OS X Server version 10.3.6 or later

You will have to decide on the amount of flexibility and expandability you would like in your setup before installing either one of these systems. If you choose to run Mac OS X on your metadata controller, you will be limited in the options for mail, AFP, SMB, FTP, Web, and other server services. Mac OS X Server is built specifically to run server services and will give you much more flexibility in managing your network. Also, ECC (error correcting code) RAM is available only on Xserve G5s and certain G5 desktops at this time, greatly increasing the reliability of your metadata controller.

Regardless of which supported Macintosh you use for your metadata controller, an Apple Fibre Channel PCI Express or PCI-X card will need to be installed in the system.

Server Applications

Apple's Xserve G5 servers will have to be configured as metadata controllers to work with Xsan. Several applications can assist you in setting up your server. These applications can be installed on any machine that is connected to your network and is visible to the metadata controller you are configuring.

The following applications are listed as Mac OS X Server Admin Tools, and can be downloaded at www.apple.com/downloads/macosx/apple:

Server Assistant: Allows setup and configuration of one or more Xserve computers. This application helps you set up servers interactively or automate setup using data saved in a file or in Open Directory.

Server Admin: Allows setup and configuration of server services such as mail, NAT, firewall, AFP, SMB, VPN, and others.

Workgroup Manager: Creates and manages groups of users and computers; manages preferences for Mac OS X users; enables network settings for Windows clients; manages share points; and accesses the Inspector, which lets you work with Open Directory entries.

Entering Xserve Firmware Boot Commands

In Xserve G5 systems with no video card (so-called headless systems), it might be necessary to start the CPU in various modes without connecting the system to a keyboard or monitor. This is especially useful when you would like to put the server in target disk mode or to startup from a CD-ROM.

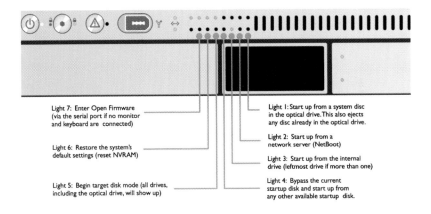

Light 7: Enter Open Firmware (via the serial port if no monitor and keyboard are connected)

Light 6: Restore the system's default settings (reset NVRAM)

Light 5: Begin target disk mode (all drives, including the optical drive, will show up)

Light 1: Start up from a system disc in the optical drive. This also ejects any disc already in the optical drive.

Light 2: Start up from a network server (NetBoot)

Light 3: Start up from the internal drive (leftmost drive if more than one)

Light 4: Bypass the current startup disk and start up from any other available startup disk.

Follow these steps to initiate a command from the front panel.

1. With the power off, press the system identifier button while you press the on/standby button.

2. Continue pressing the system identifier button until the top row of blue lights blinks sequentially.

3. Release the system identifier button. The rightmost light in the bottom row turns on. Press the button to light the next light in the bottom row, moving from right to left. Press the button again to change lights.

4. When the light for the action you want is on, press the system identifier button for at least two seconds, until all lights in the top row are on.

5. Release the button.

Setting Up Your Server with Server Assistant

Assuming that Mac OS X Server has been properly installed on your server, you will use Server Assistant to configure your headless Xserve G5. You can use an Xsan client or your MacBook Pro to configure your server. Create a network connection using DHCP, and connect this system to the server (either directly or through a switch).

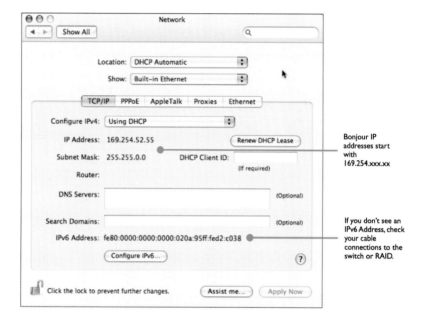

1   Run Server Assistant (Applications > Server > Server Assistant) and choose Set up a Remote Server.

    The destination window searches for all servers visible via Bonjour.

2   Select the server that you wish to configure, and enter the password in the Password field. The password will be the first eight digits of the serial number of the server. In some cases (in older servers or where the logic board has been replaced), use *12345678* as the password.

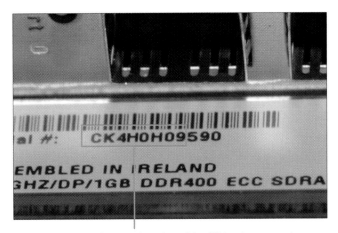

The first 8 digits of the serial number of the CPU is the password.

3   Click Continue.

You will be granted access to set up the server.

4   Choose the desired language for your server.

5   Enter the serial number for Mac OS X Server (provided in your documentation).

The Administrator Account window appears. This will be the admin for the Xserve as well as the admin for the entire SAN. Be careful when giving out this information.

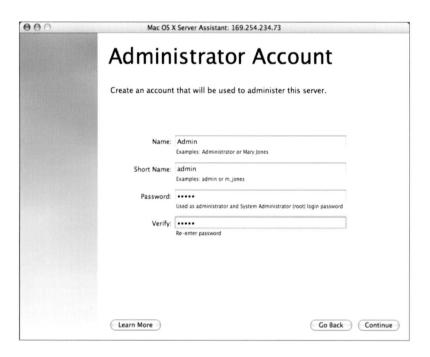

The Network Names window lets you assign what the metadata controller will be called by other controllers and clients.

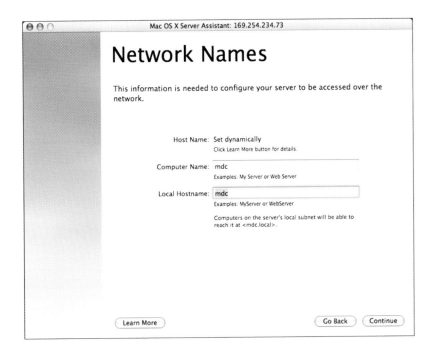

6   It is important to note that the hostname of this server will be mdc. Normally, an FQDM (fully qualified domain name) would be used here, such as www.apple.com. Since our SAN does not require access to the public Internet, and does not need to be resolved by other users, we can safely place a non-FQDM name in the Local HostName field.

7   In the Network Interfaces window, we are able to assign pro-
    tocols to physical interfaces. We will be using Built-in Ethernet
    1 for connection to the metadata network using TCP/IP proto-
    col. In the case where you are administering a separate LDAP
    server, you might want to enable TCP/IP on Built-in Ethernet 2.
    If you forget to set it up, it can always be configured after the
    server has been set up.

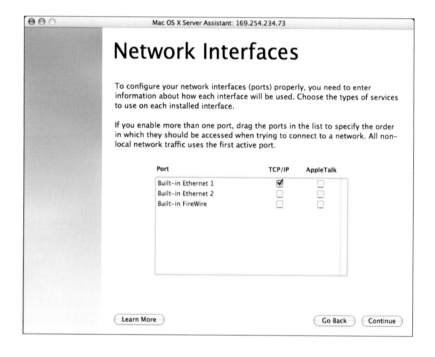

8   The next window, TCP/IP Connection, will assign the static IP
    to your metadata controller (choose Manually from the pop-up
    menu). This IP can be one of any number of supported non-
    routed IP addresses. They include:

Private Address Range	Associated Subnet Mask	Comments
10.0.0.0-10.255.255.255	255.0.0.0 - Class A	10/8
172.16.0.0-172.31.255.255	255.240.0.0 - Class B	172.16/12
192.168.0.0-192.168.255.255	255.255.0.0 - Class C	192.168/16

Here is an example of a possible implementation:

IP Address	System Name
10.1.0.1	Primary metadata controller
10.1.0.2	Secondary metadata controller
10.1.0.101	Client #1
10.1.0.102	Client #2
10.1.0.103	Client #3
10.1.0.162	Client #62

(You can have a total of 64 nodes on Xsan, thus the last client
would be client #62.)

This example uses the 10.0.0.0–10.255.255.255 address range for the metadata network.

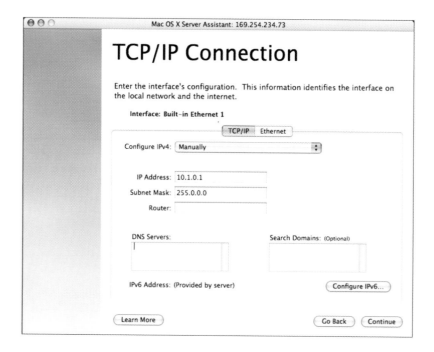

9   The Directory Usage window allows you to determine whether the server you are configuring is to be used as a stand-alone server, an Open Directory master, an Open Directory replica, or whether it is connected to a directory system.

Note: In this instance, we will not be entering a Router address for the NIC connected to the metadata network. You will receive a warning stating "The host portion of the Router Address cannot be all zeros. Do you want to cancel and make changes or continue?" Click continue to advance to the next step.

Choose Standalone Server for the directory usage. This will assume that we are not hosting a directory server on this metadata controller. If you must use this primary metadata controller as an Open Directory master, it is recommended that you choose Standalone Master. You can use Server Admin to promote the server to an Open Directory master after the server has been configured.

Note that the primary metadata controller should be running as few services as possible. This means that FTP, AFP, NFS, mail, and other services should reside on other servers. This keeps the additional network traffic to a minimum and allows the metadata controller to focus primarily on metadata token passing.

10 The Services window allows you to enable the services that you would like the server to run. One service that is extremely helpful to enable is the Apple Remote Desktop Client service. This will start the ARD service on the server so that after a restart you will be able to remotely administer your metadata controller with Apple Remote Desktop.

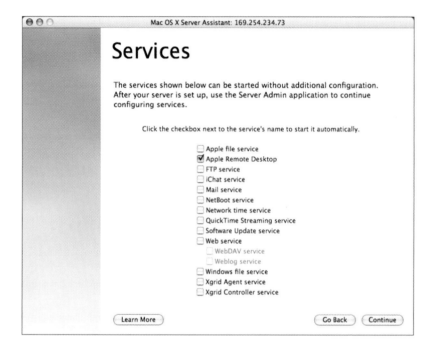

11 Confirm your settings in the next window, and you are finished with Server Assistant. The server will restart and be ready for Xsan Admin to be installed.

Configuring Xsan for Local Authentication

Local authentication is the simplest way to configure your system. It relies on the clients to locally authenticate to their own machines. Once authenticated, they are able to access the SAN volume(s) and are able to read and write to files that their UID (user ID) or GID (group ID) has access to.

There isn't much additional configuring to do on the metadata controllers if you decide to use this authentication scheme. Installing and configuring Xsan Admin will be the final step in you setup. The next chapter describes the specifics in configuring clients for local authentication.

Configuring Xsan for Open Directory

It is recommended that you use a separate server specifically dedicated to run Open Directory so that the metadata controller handles only Xsan administration issues. Running a minimum of services on the metadata controller ensures that there is no latency in the token-passing operation.

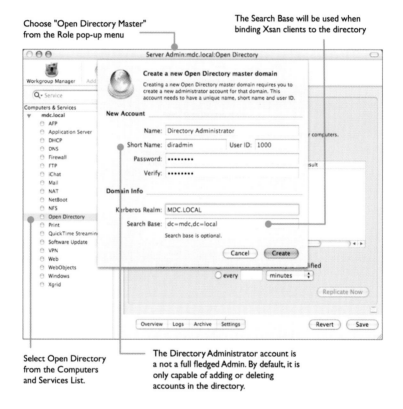

Choose "Open Directory Master" from the Role pop-up menu

The Search Base will be used when binding Xsan clients to the directory

Select Open Directory from the Computers and Services List.

The Directory Administrator account is a not a full fledged Admin. By default, it is only capable of adding or deleting accounts in the directory.

Run Server Admin to configure your server for Open Directory. You will select the service and change the server from Standalone Master to Open Directory Master. You will need to set up a separate account for the Directory Administrator.

For more information on Open Directory and other server management classes offered by Apple, visit http://training.apple.com.

Permissions with Centralized Directories

When all of the users are centralized in a directory, their user IDs are different by default. This allows the SAN to differentiate each client by their user ID and to determine appropriate permissions.

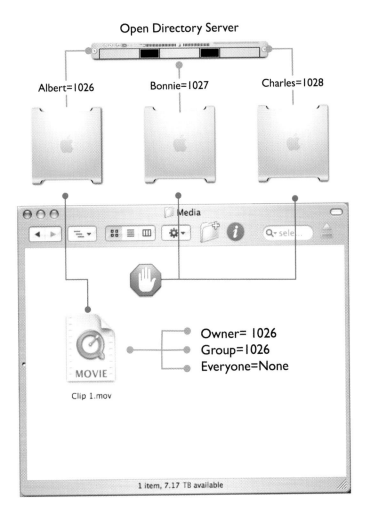

Home Directories

When using Final Cut Pro on your SAN, it is important to make sure your user's home directory remains on the local client machine. This is not a problem with local authentication. When using a centralized directory however, you will have the option of placing the user's home directory on the SAN volume. This is not recommended for Final Cut Pro.

To resolve this, use Workgroup Manager to create a Home folder for a centralized user on a local volume. The following is an example of how you would set it up for the user Albert.

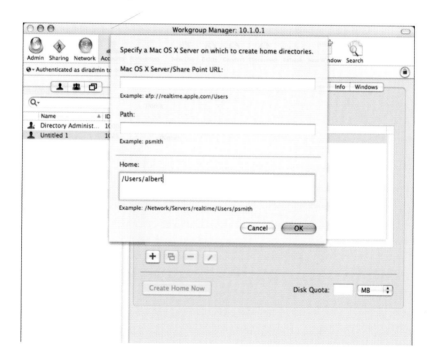

Sharing Your SAN over Ethernet

In cases where direct Fibre Channel access to the SAN is not available or desired from your clients, it is possible to use File Sharing Services such as AFP or SNB to reshare the volume or portions of the SAN volume over Ethernet. Remember that the file server must be directly connected via Fibre Channel to the SAN in order to reshare out files over Ethernet. Use Server Admin (Applications/Server) to configure and enable sharing services on the File Sharing Server.

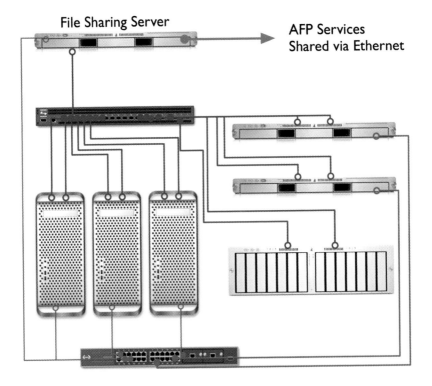

File Sharing Server

AFP Services
Shared via Ethernet

File Sharing Tested Maximums

Component	Maximum	Tested Maximum
AFP server	Number of connected users	1000
AFP server	Shareable volume size	16 TB
AFP server	Number of files per volume	250 million
AFP server	Number of share points	255
SMB server	Number of open files	1,000
SMB server	Number of connected users	1,000

6

Setting Up Your Clients

Xsan can have up to 64 clients all sharing up to eight volumes. Remember that metadata controllers also count as client systems accessing the SAN. Realistically, that means up to 62 editors can be editing material, and two Xserve G5 metadata controllers will be hosting the volume(s).

There are two general ways to build your SAN:

- NetInfo: In this implementation, client nodes are locally authenticated. This means that clients log in to their local directory, and each individual system is in charge of granting access to its own CPUs. The benefit to this implementation is that it is fairly easy to configure, but it is viable only on small SANs of up to six clients. As the SAN grows in size, a NetInfo-configured SAN can be difficult to manage. This is because all users should have consistent user IDs. Since there is no centralized directory, the NetInfo database must essentially be "cloned" on all client systems as the number of users increases.

- Centralized directory: A centralized directory, such as Open Directory, allows the user database to be centralized in one location. Since the authentication occurs on the server, all clients must be bound to the server and able to access the common directory. When a user logs in to a client machine, the user name and password are verified with the server1, and the user is granted access to the local computer. This method also allows for unique user IDs as well as making it simple to add users as the SAN grows in size.

G5 PCI Slot Configuration

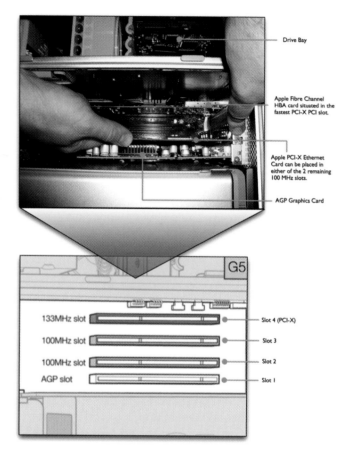

Newer G5 desktops have three open PCI Express slots. Slot 3 is an 8x slot, and slots 2 and 4 are 4x slots.

Slot 1 is a 16x slot and is used by the included graphics card. All 4 slots have 16 lane connectors.

For newer G5s, you should place the Apple Fibre Channel PCI Express card in slot 2 or 4, and leave slot 3 open for higher-bandwidth video capture cards.

Permissions with Local Authentication

In configurations where you will be authenticating to local client machines, the order in which the user is added determines the UID (user ID) and GID (group ID) for that user. The SAN volume follows the UID/GID only when determining access to files and folders. This means that three clients might have conflicting UIDs and be given read/write access to the same file or folder. This may be desired, but it can cause problems if two users write to the same project simultaneously.

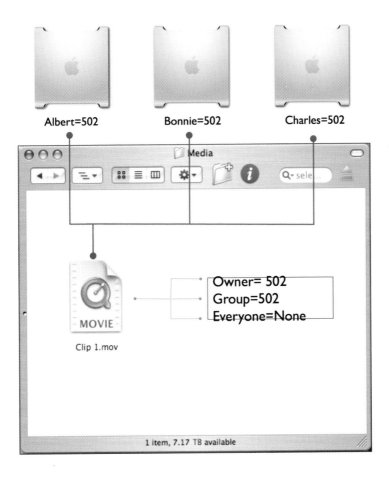

User ID Setup

Since the UID and GID are automatically assigned when you create a new user on a local machine (System Preferences > Accounts), you will need a way to replicate the UID information across all local client machines. This will make it easier for the SAN to resolve UIDs to actual named users accessing the SAN.

The main way to make sure UIDs are identical across your SAN client nodes is to create all users in the exact same order on all machines. This will insure that Albert, for example, is assigned a UID of 502 (the first Admin user is assigned 501 at initial configuration). Bonnie, the second user created, will be assigned a UID of 503. If you are consistent across all machines, you will have replicated the user list properly.

Viewing and Changing the UID and Group ID

You can use the NetInfo Manager application to view and update the user and group ID for any user.

Changing the UID is helpful, for example, if two users have conflicting UID numbers and you must change one of them. Updating this information requires two steps:

1. Change the UID and GID in NetInfo Manager (Applications > Utilities > NetInfo Manager).

2. Update the permissions of the users previously created Home folder by using the Terminal application (Applications > Utilities > Terminal).

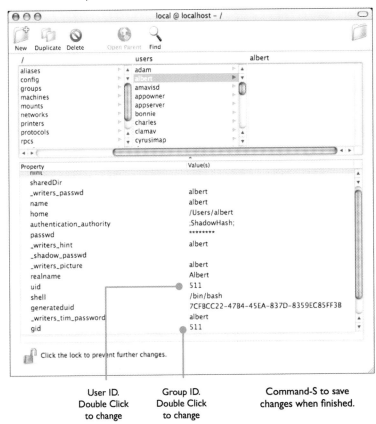

Changing Home Folder Ownership

If you have to change the UID and GID of a user, you will have to update the ownership of their previously created Home folder (Users > *username*). If this information is not updated, the user will not have access to his or her own Home folder. This modification is done in the Terminal.

1   Run the Terminal application (Applications > Utilities > Terminal).

2   Change the directory to the Users directory:

```
$ cd /Users
$ ls -l
```

This will give a detailed list of the folders as well as user and group information.

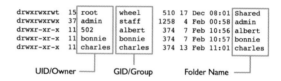

drwxrwxrwt	15	root	wheel	510	17	Dec	08:01	Shared
drwxrwxrwx	37	admin	staff	1258	4	Feb	00:58	admin
drwxr-xr-x	11	502	albert	374	7	Feb	10:56	albert
drwxr-xr-x	11	bonnie	bonnie	374	7	Feb	10:57	bonnie
drwxr-xr-x	11	charles	charles	374	13	Feb	11:01	charles

UID/Owner ─┘   GID/Group   Folder Name ─┘

Notice that Albert's UID says 502 instead of his proper name. This is because Albert has been changed to UID 511 in NetInfo Manager. The user with ID 502 now has ownership of /Users/albert, and not Albert himself. Let's fix that:

3   Type the following:

```
$ sudo chown -R albert:albert /Users/albert
```

Change ownership command ─┘   New owner/ UID   New Group/ GID   File or folder being modified

Enter an admin password, and the folder and its contents will be modified. The `chown` command changes ownership of files or folders. The `-R` option changes the ownership of the file hierarchies as well. You can do a `ls -l` to verify that Albert now is the owner of his folder.

Setting Up Groups (Centralized Directory)

When configuring a centralized directory, all of the clients authenticate through the server. In Server Admin, the Open Directory service will be promoted from Standalone Server to Open Directory Master. Once enabled, the user and group list can be configured in Workgroup Manager. The group list will allow you to place one or more users in a particular group, giving you control over numerous parameters for a given set of users.

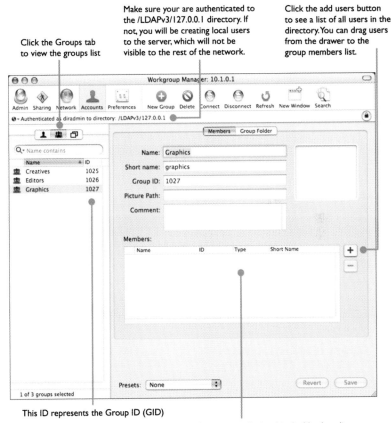

Click the Groups tab to view the groups list

Make sure your are authenticated to the /LDAPv3/127.0.0.1 directory. If not, you will be creating local users to the server, which will not be visible to the rest of the network.

Click the add users button to see a list of all users in the directory. You can drag users from the drawer to the group members list.

This ID represents the Group ID (GID)

All members of a group are displayed in the Members list

Setting Up Users (Centralized Directory)

As clients log into the directory, they will have to enter a username and password to access their local machine. This centralized list of users is stored and managed on the LDAP server using Workgroup Manager.

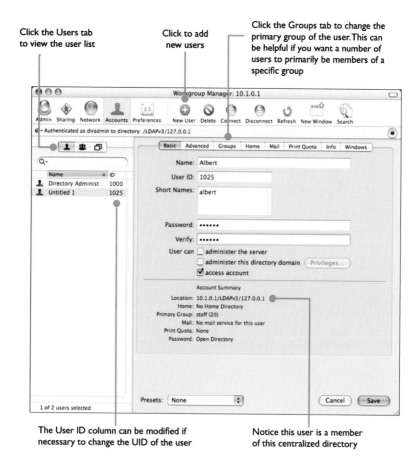

Click the Users tab to view the user list

Click to add new users

Click the Groups tab to change the primary group of the user. This can be helpful if you want a number of users to primarily be members of a specific group

The User ID column can be modified if necessary to change the UID of the user

Notice this user is a member of this centralized directory

Setting Up Primary Groups (Centralized Directory)

Click the Groups tab to change view and modify the primary and 'Other Groups' for this user.

Drag the desired primary group from the Groups list on the right into the Short Name of the User. This will change the users primary group to the newly added group.

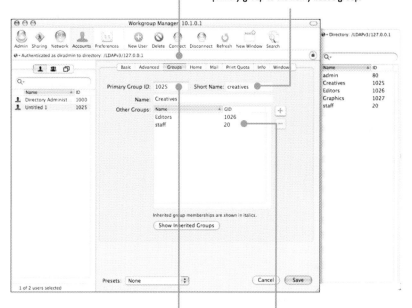

This new primary group ID means that any folders created by this user will be accessible to the 'Creatives' group by default.

Although this users primary group is no longer staff, the staff group has been added to the Other Groups list so that folders owned by the staff group are accessible by this user.

Binding a Client to the Directory

Using Directory Access (Applications > Utilities) you can bind a client to a centralized directory such as Open Directory.

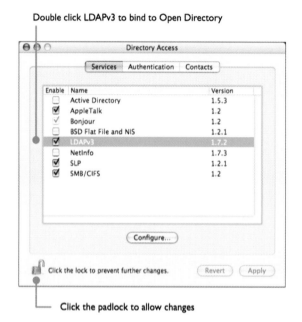

Double click LDAPv3 to bind to Open Directory

Click the padlock to allow changes

Creating a Directory Entry

You can disable the 'Use for
contacts' option if you are not using
the LDAP server for contact lookup

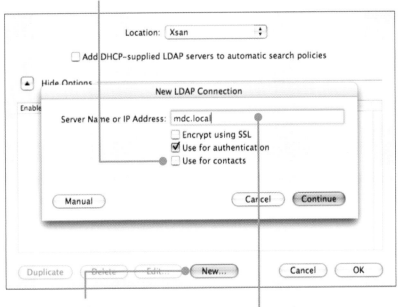

Click the New button to create a
new LDAP connection

Enter the Bonjour name, FQDN or
IP address of the directory server

Setting Up Your Clients

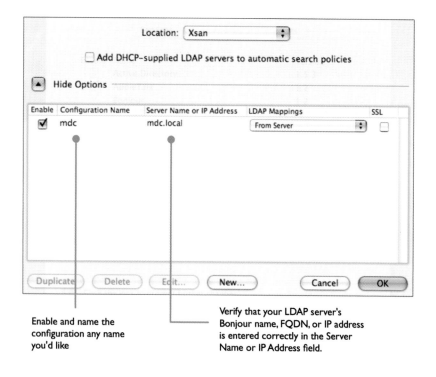

Location: Xsan

☐ Add DHCP-supplied LDAP servers to automatic search policies

▲ Hide Options

Enable	Configuration Name	Server Name or IP Address	LDAP Mappings	SSL
☑	mdc	mdc.local	From Server	☐

(Duplicate) (Delete) (Edit...) (New...)   (Cancel) (OK)

Enable and name the
configuration any name
you'd like

Verify that your LDAP server's
Bonjour name, FQDN, or IP address
is entered correctly in the Server
Name or IP Address field.

78

Checking for Successful Client Binding

You can enter the Terminal Application (Applications > Utilities) and check for a successful client binding.

Type the following:

```
$ lookupd -d
> userWithName: albert
```

Enter the username of any user in your central directory. In this case, albert. If you are not bound, you will get a return of "nil." If your binding was successful, you will see the following:

```
Dictionary: "DS: user albert"
_lookup_agent: DSAgent
_lookup_validation: 1108602456
gid: 1026
home: /Users/albert
name: albert Albert
passwd: ******** ********
realname: Albert
shell: /bin/bash
uid: 1025
+ Category: user
+ Time to live: 43200
+ Age: 0 (expires in 43200 seconds)
+ Negative: No
+ Cache hits: 0
+ Retain count
```

7 Fibre Channel Networking

Fibre Channel is the protocol used for data transfer due to its high speed and provisions for high availability. It is essentially the classic SCSI protocol, mixed with an address-based networking system, so that multiple hosts can be online and request and send data to and from storage devices.

A speed of 2 Gbits per second is used with all Xsan elements, which yields a theoretical limit of 200 MB/s for transmission and reception, for a total of 400 MB/s per cable.

There are two kinds of entities in Fibre Channel networking:

- Initiators are end-user computers and servers that receive data from and transmit data to storage.

- Targets are storage arrays and tape drives that transmit data to and receive data from initiators.

Fibre Channel Protocols

There are three protocols used with Fibre Channel networking:

- Point-to-Point protocol is used when connecting storage directly to the host. Only two devices are involved.

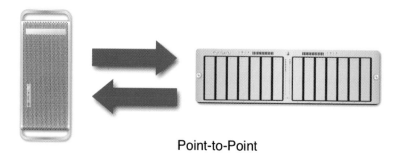

Point-to-Point

- Arbitrated loop protocol works as a "party line" for all of the entities on the network. Regardless of the number of connected devices, only two devices can communicate at any one moment. An 8-bit addressing system is used to route data from one entity to another.

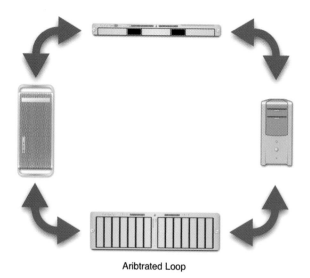

Aribtrated Loop

- Fabric switches are similar to Ethernet switches, in that multiple communications can be occurring on the switch—as many as are needed at any given moment. A 24-bit addressing system is used to route data from one entity to another.

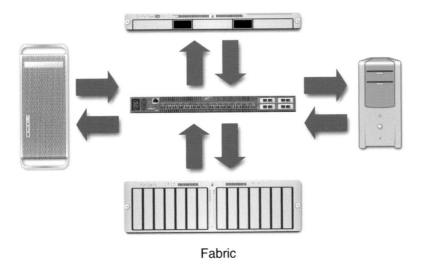

Fabric

Fabric Topologies

When planning your SAN, you might require more than one switch to accommodate all of the entities. The following topologies are used to interconnect fabric switches:

- A cascade topology interconnects two switches, using two or more cables connected to ports on each switch. More than one interconnecting cable is used to increase the bandwidth of data transferred and to provide redundancy in case any one connection goes down.

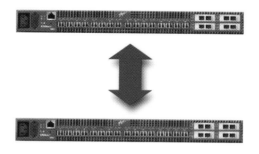

Cascade

- Cascade loop topology is used for three or more switches, where the first and last switch are further interconnected. This allows data to follow the "first or shortest path first" (FSPF) rule, a standard function of fabric protocol.

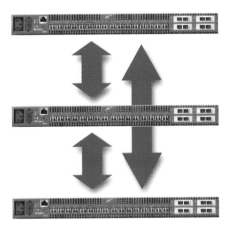

Cascade Loop

- Mesh topology has each switch fully interconnected to every other switch. This allows for greatest efficiency and redundancy in the fabric.

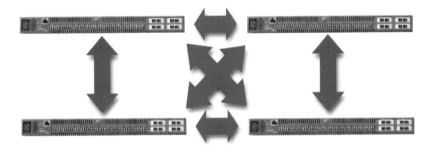

Mesh

Fibre Channel Host Bus Adapters (HBAs)

Apple's Fibre Channel PCI Express and 133 MHz PCI-X HBA is used in Xsan integration. At $599 ($499 for the PCI-X Fibre Channel HBA), it is often as much as $2,000 less than equivalent products from other manufacturers, and comes with two 2.9 m copper cables. This card has two small form factor pluggable (SFP) ports.

Fibre Channel Cabling

Copper Cabling

Two 2.9 m copper cables come standard with each Fibre Channel HBA. SFP transceivers are already attached to each end. Copper cables of longer lengths should be avoided with Xsan.

Optical Cabling

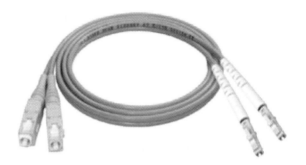

Use 2 Gbits/s LC cable. These cables usually have bright orange jacketing, although multiple-color cables are emerging on the market. Check the printing on the cable's jacketing to be sure of its specifications.

Cable lengths depend on substrate size ("the smaller the diameter, the longer the run"):

Cable Size	Run Length	SFP Transceiver Required
62.5 μ	300 m	Short wavelength (short haul)
50 μ	500 m	Short wavelength (short haul)
9 μ	10 km	Long wavelength (long haul)

Prefabricated optical cables are the easiest to implement, as cable ends are already finely polished to interface with the SFP transceiver. Lengths vary from 1 m to 500 m.

Optical cable is manufactured from fiberglass substrate. It is therefore extremely fragile. When running Fibre cable from the core SAN components, take great care not to bend or kink the cable. As often as possible, lay it into conduit, rather than pulling it through.

SFP Transceivers for Optical Cables

Two SFP transceivers are needed for each optical cable used in your integration. Apple recommends the following manufacturers and part numbers.

Short wavelength (short haul)

- Finisar FTRJ-8519-P1BNL
- Pico Light PL-XPL-VE-S24-11
- Pico Light PL-XPL-VC-S23-11
- JDS Uniphase JSM-21S0AA1
- JDS Uniphase JSP-21S0AA1

Long wavelength (long haul)

- Finisar FTRJ-1319-P1BTL

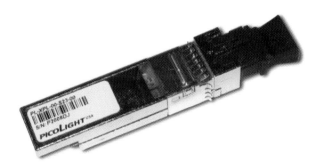

Most Xserve RAID controllers have SFP connectors as well. However, first-generation Xserve RAIDs have HSSDC2 connectors instead. Those connectors look quite different from SFP ports.

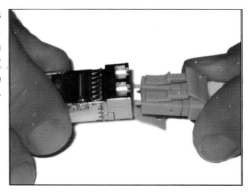

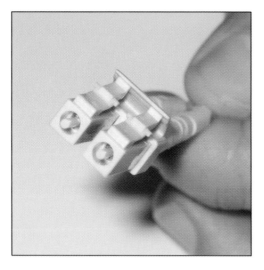

Usually those RAIDs were sold with copper cables that have HSSDC2 connectors on one end and SFP connectors on the other. Use those cables to connect the controllers to the switch. There are no issues with using HSSDC2-ported controllers.

Switch Configuration Basics

All switches approved for use with Xsan have auto-sensing SFP ports. Most can suppress registered state name changes (RSCN) on ports that will be attached to the initiator nodes (clients or controllers) of the SAN. This allows uninterrupted communication between the nodes and the storage if any of the nodes are started up or are restarted during SAN activity.

Brocade

Currently supported switches for Xsan:

- SilkWorm 3200 or 3250 8-port fabric switch
- SilkWorm 3800 or 3850 16-port fabric switch
- SilkWorm 3900 32-port fabric switch
- SilkWorm 12000 64-port dual-domain director

Administration

All Brocade switches can be administered through a built-in Web host called Web Tools. The full documentation for this interface is provided on a CD-ROM that comes with each switch.

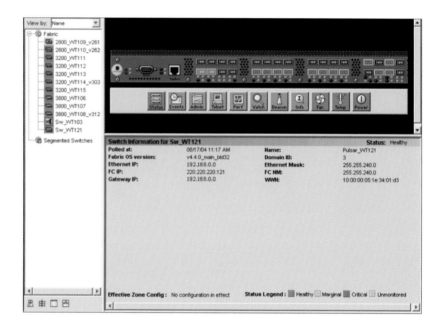

Out of the box, the switch can be contacted by pointing a browser to the following:

IP address: 10.77.77.77

Netmask: 255.0.0.0

Gateway: 0.0.0.0

Username: admin

Password: password

On first launch, Brocade's Web Tools requires a license. Have the license ready and follow the onscreen instructions to install the license. You will then be prompted to select a new username and password.

To reboot the switch:

1. Select the desired switch from the Fabric Tree.

   The selected switch appears in the Switch view.

2. Select the Admin icon from the Switch view.

   The login dialog appears.

3. Enter the admin username and password.

4. Click the Firmware tab.

5. Click the Reboot radio button.

6. Click Apply.

To download a new version of the firmware:

1. Select the desired switch from the Fabric Tree.

   The selected switch appears in the Switch view.

2. Select the Admin icon from the Switch view.

   The login dialog appears.

3. Enter the admin username and password.

4. Click the Firmware tab.

5. Click the Firmware Download radio button.

6. Enter the username, password, and host IP information.

7. Enter the fully qualified path to the filename.

8. Click Apply.

To suppress RSCN on initiator ports:

Brocade does not offer a RSCN suppression feature. To inhibit RSCN interruptions when client computers are booted or restarted, separate "mini" zones for each client and the storage must be created. Refer to the documentation that came with your Brocade switch to set up these zones.

To create inter-switch links:

Brocade refers to inter-switch linking as ISL trunking.

1. Select the desired switch from the Fabric Tree.

   The selected switch appears in the Switch view.

2. Click the Admin icon from the Switch view.

   The login dialog appears.

3. Enter the admin username and password.

4. Click the Port Setting tab.

5. For SilkWorm 12000 and 24000 switches: Select the slot subtab that corresponds to the correct slot for the logical switch.

6. To enable trunking mode on a port, select the box in the Enable Trunking column that corresponds to the port you wish to trunk. To disable trunking mode on a port, deselect the box.

7. Click Apply.

Brocade contact information:

www.brocade.com

Corporate	(408) 333-8000
Tech support	(888) 283-4273
	(408) 333-6061
Europe	+800 28 34 27 33
Tech support:	support@brocade.com

Emulex

Currently supported switches for Xsan:

- InSpeed 355 12-port arbitrated loop switch
- InSpeed 375 20-port arbitrated loop switch

Full documentation for these switches, including special setup guides for Apple-based implementations, is available at www.emulex.com/ts/indexemu.html.

Administration

Emulex switches can be administered through a built-in Web host called Web Manager.

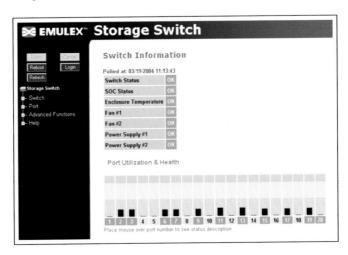

Out of the box, the switch can be contacted by pointing a browser to the following:

IP address: 169.254.10.10
Netmask: 255.255.0.0
Gateway: 0.0.0.0
Password: password

To reboot the switch:

1.   On the main page of the Web Manager, click the Reboot button.

To suppress RSCN on initiator ports

1.   On the left side of the interface, choose Port > Smart Settings.

2.   Select the "Initiator with Stealth" Smart Setting from the list box.

3.   From the list of port numbers, select the ports that will use the selected Smart Setting under the Assign heading. *Remember to select only initiator ports for this setting.*

4.   Click Submit to save the settings.

To upgrade firmware:

1.   On the left side of the interface, choose Help > Downloads.

     The Emulex Web site appears.

2.   Click the "drivers, software, and manuals" link, and select the switch product model under the "drivers, software, and manuals by product model number" section.

3.   Under Download New Alternate Firmware Version to Switch, choose Browse to navigate to and select the appropriate file on the Mac.

     The file must have a .bin extension.

4.   Click Start to load the new firmware image.

5.   Once the firmware has been installed, the new firmware should appear as the AlternateVersion firmware.

6.   Under Next Boot Firmware Version, ensure that the "Use Alternate Version on Next Reboot" option is selected.

     The alternate firmware version currently displayed will be loaded on the next boot cycle.

7.   Click Reboot to reset the switch using the selected firmware.

To create inter-switch links:

Emulex refers to inter-switch linking as trunking.

Ports designated for trunking must be assigned to a Trunk Group.

1. On the left side of the interface, choose Advanced Functions > Automatic Trunking.

   The Automatic Trunking page appears.

2. Select a trunk group for each port by clicking the appropriate trunk group option.

3. When you are finished making changes, click Submit.

Emulex contact information:

www.emulex.com

Corporate	(800) 368-5391
	(714) 662-5600
	(714) 241-0792 (fax)
Tech support	(800) 854-7112
	(714) 885-3402
General information:	info@emulex.com
Tech support:	emailsupport@emulex.com
Repair:	repair@emulex.com

QLogic

Currently supported switches for QLogic:

- SANbox 2-8 8-port fabric switch
- SANbox 2-16 16-port fabric switch
- SANbox 2-64 64-port fabric switch
- SANbox 5200 or 5202 8 to 20-port scalable, stackable fabric switch

Qlogic switches should ship with 5.0 or greater firmware, which is compatible with Xsan. If you happen to receive a switch with older firmware, use the Qlogic SANSurfer Switch Manager software and refer to the following section on upgrading firmware to upgrade the firmware.

Administration

Default settings for use with SANbox Manager:

IP address: 10.0.0.1

Netmask: 255.0.0.0

Gateway: 10.0.0.254

Username: admin

Password: password

To connect to the switch:

1. Launch Safari and enter the IP address of the switch.

2. Choose Open Existing Fabric and click Proceed.

   A login window appears.

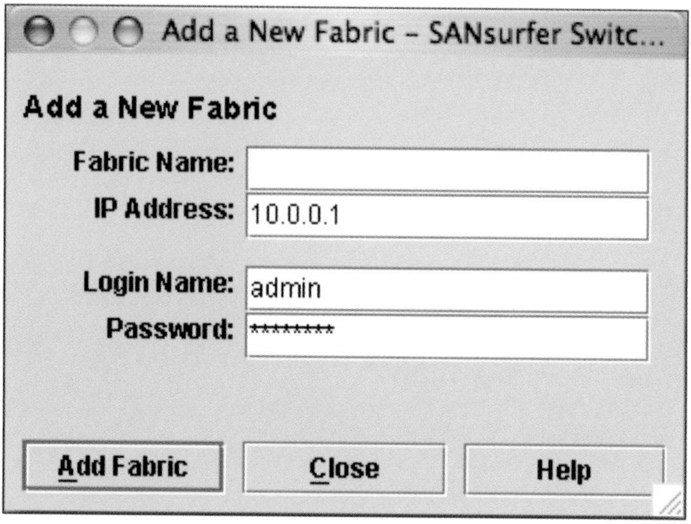

⊖ ○ ⊖ Add a New Fabric – SANsurfer Switc...

Add a New Fabric

Fabric Name:	
IP Address:	10.0.0.1
Login Name:	admin
Password:	********

| **Add Fabric** | **Close** | **Help** |

---

3. If connecting for the first time, enter 10.0.0.1 in the IP Address field, *admin* in the Login Name field, and *password* in the Password field.

   After a short pause, the main Fabric view appears.

4 Double-click the image of your switch to observe current port states and to further administer the switch. This view is called the Faceplate.

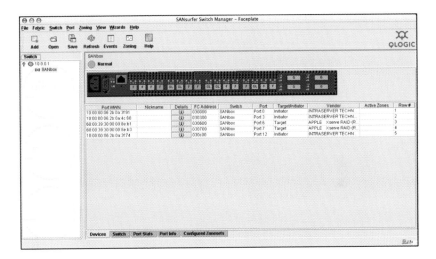

To reboot the switch:

1 In Faceplate view, choose Switch > Reset Switch.

There are three reset options:

- Hot Reset simply allows a reset during communications, to incorporate new firmware.

- Reset forces the switch to run its power on self-test (POST).

- Hard Reset forces the switch to factory default settings and forces a POST.

To suppress RSCN on initiator ports:

1. In Faceplate view, select the icons for each initiator port on which you wish to suppress RSCN.

2. Choose Port > Port Properties 1G/2G.

   A window appears, allowing you to change the properties of the port(s) you've selected.

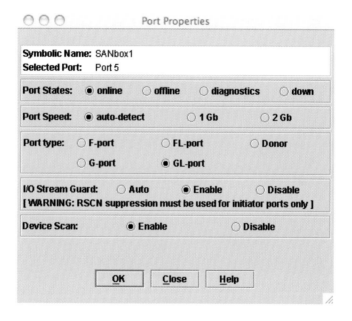

3. In the I/O Stream Guard section near the bottom, click the Enable radio button. Remember to select only initiator ports for this setting.

4. In the Device Scan section at the bottom, click the Disable radio button. Remember to select only initiator ports for this setting.

5. Click OK.

   A confirmation is given once the ports have been set.

6. Click OK.

To upgrade firmware:

1. In Faceplate view, choose Switch > Load Firmware

   A window appears prompting you to browse for the firmware file.

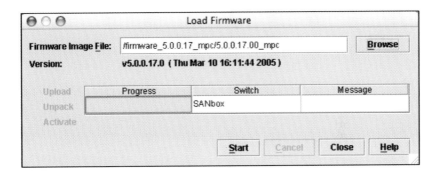

2. Click Select, and browse to the firmware file.

3. Click Choose.

4. In the original window, click the Start button.

   The firmware uploads to the switch. You will then be prompted to activate the firmware.

5. Click Yes to activate the firmware.

To create inter-switch links:

1. Simply connect two switches with cables. The ports will auto-negotiate to E (expansion) ports.

2. If the port status lights on the switch remain blinking, it usually means that the two switches being linked have the same domain number. Simply power down and power up one of the switches. When it restarts, it will auto-negotiate to a new domain number.

To connect to the switch when the IP address is not known:

1. Unplug the switch from its power supply

2. Take a paperclip and insert it into the reset hole on the front of the switch underneath the Ethernet port. Hold the paper clip while you power up the switch.

3. Wait 10 seconds, then release the paperclip.

   The switch can now be accessed via Telnet.

   Temporary IP address: 10.0.0.1

   Login: prom

   Password: prom

   You are now able to connect to the switch and perform a reset of its parameters via a Telnet connection.

QLogic contact information:

www.qlogic.com

Corporate	(800) 662-4771
	(949) 389-6000
	(949) 389-6009 (fax)
Tech support	(952) 932-4040
General information:	www.qlogic.com/buyqlogic/contact_sales.asp
Tech support:	support@qlogic.com
Technical training:	tech.training@qlogic.com

Cisco MDS 9000 Series

Cisco contact information:

www.cisco.com

Corporate   (800) 553-6387
                 (408) 526-4000
Tech support   (800) 553-2447
                 (408) 526-7209
Tech support:
www.cisco.com/warp/public/687/Directory/DirTAC.shtml
www.cisco.com/public/support/tac/contacts.shtml
Training/certification information:
www.cisco.com/go/certsupport

8 Xsan Admin Configuration

Let's look at the steps to get Xsan up and running:

1. Set up the Fibre Channel network.
2. Set up the Ethernet network.
3. Set up SAN users and groups.
4. Set up RAID arrays.
5. Install Xsan software on all SAN computers (servers and clients).
6. Shut down all components. Power up (in this order) switches, storage, servers, and clients.
7. Log in to the SAN.
8. Choose a controller and add clients.
9. Label and initialize available LUNs.
10. Create volumes.
11. Add storage pools to volumes.
12. Add LUNs to storage pools.
13. Set up status notifications (optional).
14. Assign folders to storage pools (optional).
15. Set user and group quotas (optional).
16. Start the volumes and mount them on clients.

Logging Into Your Metadata Controller

Enter the IP address of a metadata controller. You can also enter in the Bonjour name such as mdc.local.

Enter an administrator's User Name.

Enter the password, and check if you would like it added to your system's keychain.

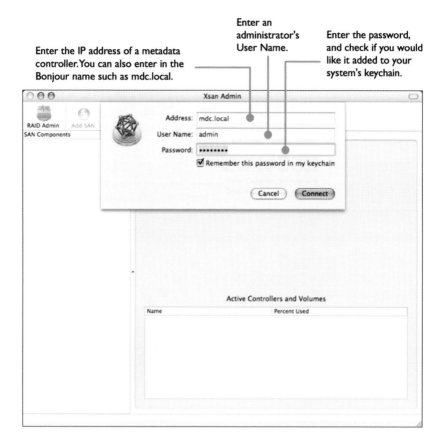

Adding Xsan Clients

The IP or name of the SAN.

The metadata controller has not been authenticated, and is waiting for a serial number to be entered.

Set up will allow you to setup your Computers, LUNs, Storage, and Notifications.

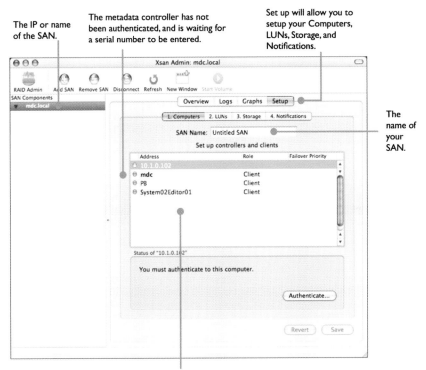

The name of your SAN.

IP addresses will show up in the list for a moment, with a grey status dot. When you authenticate using an administrator name and password, Xsan will retrieve the computer's Bonjour name, and the status dot will progress to orange. The Bonjour name of a client can be found in System Preferences > Sharing.

Setting Up the Controller

Assign the role of this computer – a metadata controller or client.

Enter the serial number for each client of the SAN. Click the Validate button after entering the serial number to make sure the number is a valid serial number for the version of Xsan you are running.

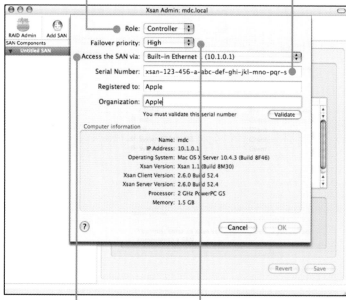

On controllers, if multiple network interfaces are detected, you can choose the NIC you would like the metadata network to communicate on.

Assign each controller either a High, Medium, or Low failover. This determines the priority of failover if the primary controller fails.

Setting Up the Clients

The name of the SAN appears in the components list after it has been entered and saved in the SAN Name field.

If you don't see all of your clients, click Refresh.

The computer that is bold in the list represents the metadata controller that currently is hosting the SAN.

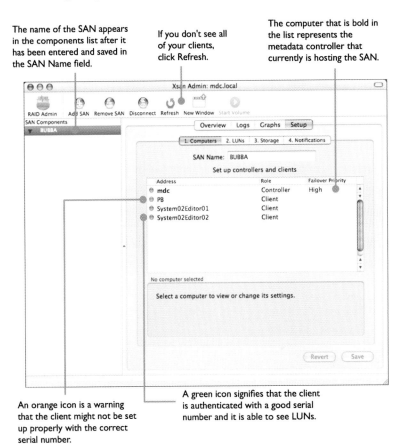

An orange icon is a warning that the client might not be set up properly with the correct serial number.

A green icon signifies that the client is authenticated with a good serial number and it is able to see LUNs.

Labeling Your LUNs

Click the LUNs tab to view all visible
LUNs on the Fibre Channel network.

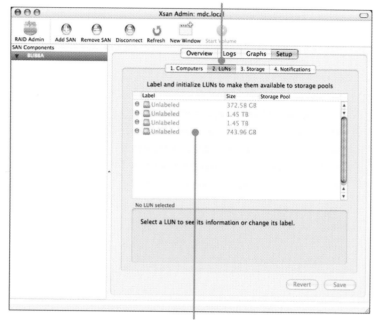

All LUNs appear in the list as Unlabeled LUNs. Double-
click each LUN to label it for use with Xsan.

Enter the name of the LUN in the Disk Name field.

Label: MDJ_LUN

LUN Information

Sectors: 781,367,296
Sector Size: 512 Bytes
Capacity: 372.58 GB
Dev Name: /dev/rdisk1
LUN ID: 0
WWN: 50:00:39:30:00:00:8E:B3:0
Inquiry String: APPLE Xserve RAID   1.50

(?)   (Cancel)   (OK)

The World Wide Name of this LUN refers to the controller that created it. This controller can be cross-referenced to the actual physical controller by using the Fibre Channel tab in the RAID Admin application.

The last digit in the World Wide Name represents the Logical Unit Number, or LUN, as it was assigned by the controller. In this case, a 0 means that this is the first LUN assigned by this controller. Unique numbers are assigned to each RAID set that appears on one side of an Xserve RAID. Further, if a RAID set is sliced, each slice will receive its own LUN ID.

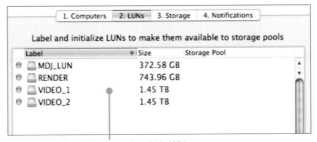

1. Computers   2. LUNs   3. Storage   4. Notifications

Label and initialize LUNs to make them available to storage pools

Label	Size	Storage Pool
⊖ ▢ MDJ_LUN	372.58 GB	
⊖ ▢ RENDER	743.96 GB	
⊖ ▢ VIDEO_1	1.45 TB	
⊖ ▢ VIDEO_2	1.45 TB	

After LUN naming, all available LUNs should show up properly in the list with a green icon on the left.

Creating Volumes

Enter the Volume name here – up to 70 characters in length. This name cannot be changed later without reinitializing the volume, so be certain of the name you'd like.

Click the Volume icon to create and name the Volume Name.

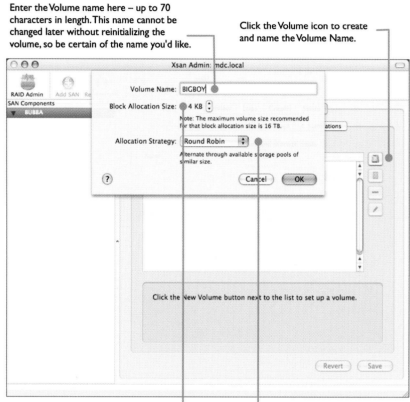

The default file system block allocation size (4 KB) is adequate for most volumes. However, you can adjust this value along with the stripe breadth of the volume's storage pools to tune performance for special applications.

Allocation strategy determines how the data is written to the available pools.

Allocation Strategies

Three allocation strategies determine how storage pools receive data within the volume (for data not assigned an affinity).

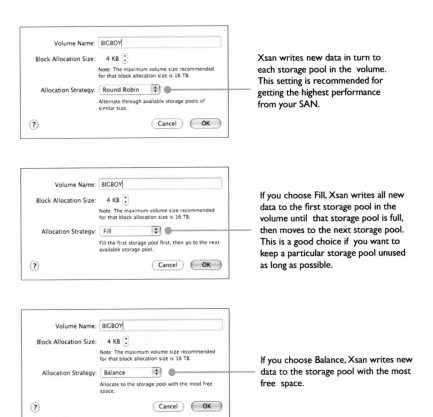

Xsan writes new data in turn to each storage pool in the volume. This setting is recommended for getting the highest performance from your SAN.

If you choose Fill, Xsan writes all new data to the first storage pool in the volume until that storage pool is full, then moves to the next storage pool. This is a good choice if you want to keep a particular storage pool unused as long as possible.

If you choose Balance, Xsan writes new data to the storage pool with the most free space.

Creating Storage Pools

Name the pool – up to 255 characters. Check
the reserved names table for a list of names
that are not available for you to use.

Click the Create Pool icon.

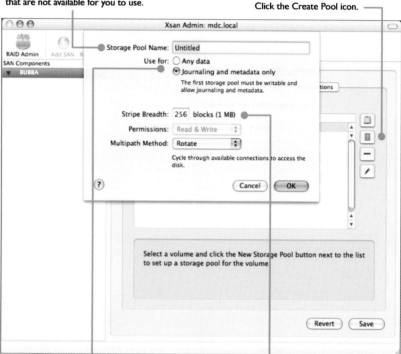

The first storage pool must contain the
journaling and metadata. You can also
choose "Any data," as this option will
place metadata and journaling info as
well as user data onto the pool.

The stripe breadth of a storage pool is the number of
file allocation blocks that are written to a LUN in the
pool before moving to the next LUN. The most efficient
data transfer size of Xserve RAID units is 1 MB. This
means that the stripe breadth is equal to 1,048,576
divided by the block allocation size. In this case, we are
using a 4K block size, so 256 blocks for the stripe
breadth is optimized for this volume.

Storage Pool Settings

Additional pools can be set to "User data only," which will not place any metadata or journaling information onto that pool.

To allow only files saved in a folder that has an affinity for this storage pool, enable "Only data with affinity."

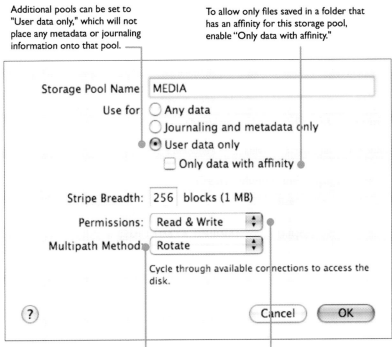

Storage Pool Name: MEDIA

Use for:
- ○ Any data
- ○ Journaling and metadata only
- ● User data only
  - ☐ Only data with affinity

Stripe Breadth: 256 blocks (1 MB)

Permissions: Read & Write ⬍

Multipath Method: Rotate ⬍

Cycle through available connections to access the disk.

(?)   (Cancel)   (OK)

If you have two Fibre Channel connections between each client computer and Xserve RAID system, choose how Xsan uses the connections. Choose Rotate to have Xsan alternate between the connections for maximum throughput. Choose Static to have Xsan assign each LUN in the storage pool alternately to one of the connections when the volume is mounted.

To prevent users from modifying the contents of the storage pool, change to Read Only.

117

Adding LUNs to Storage Pools

Drag the LUNs from the list to the right into the desired pool. You can add up to 32 LUNs per storage pool.

Select any LUN and press the Delete key to remove it from its pool and place it back into the available LUN list.

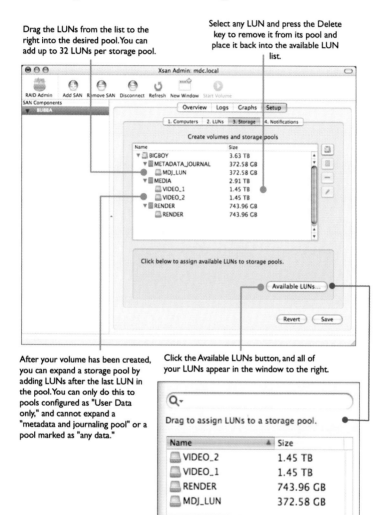

After your volume has been created, you can expand a storage pool by adding LUNs after the last LUN in the pool. You can only do this to pools configured as "User Data only," and cannot expand a "metadata and journaling pool" or a pool marked as "any data."

Click the Available LUNs button, and all of your LUNs appear in the window to the right.

Correlating LUNs to RAID Controllers

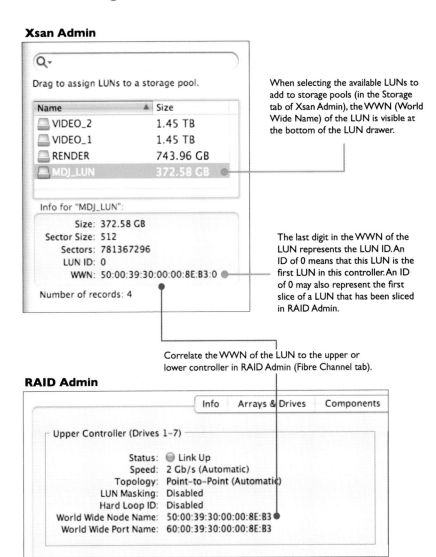

Xsan Admin

Drag to assign LUNs to a storage pool.

Name	Size
VIDEO_2	1.45 TB
VIDEO_1	1.45 TB
RENDER	743.96 GB
MDJ_LUN	372.58 GB

Info for "MDJ_LUN":

Size: 372.58 GB
Sector Size: 512
Sectors: 781367296
LUN ID: 0
WWN: 50:00:39:30:00:00:8E:B3:0

Number of records: 4

When selecting the available LUNs to add to storage pools (in the Storage tab of Xsan Admin), the WWN (World Wide Name) of the LUN is visible at the bottom of the LUN drawer.

The last digit in the WWN of the LUN represents the LUN ID. An ID of 0 means that this LUN is the first LUN in this controller. An ID of 0 may also represent the first slice of a LUN that has been sliced in RAID Admin.

Correlate the WWN of the LUN to the upper or lower controller in RAID Admin (Fibre Channel tab).

RAID Admin

Info   Arrays & Drives   Components

Upper Controller (Drives 1-7)

Status: Link Up
Speed: 2 Gb/s (Automatic)
Topology: Point-to-Point (Automatic)
LUN Masking: Disabled
Hard Loop ID: Disabled
World Wide Node Name: 50:00:39:30:00:00:8E:B3
World Wide Port Name: 60:00:39:30:00:00:8E:B3

Affinities and Permissions

In order to assign affinities to root-level folders, as well as change the owner, group, or other permissions, the volume must be mounted on the metadata controller you are connected to with Xsan Admin.

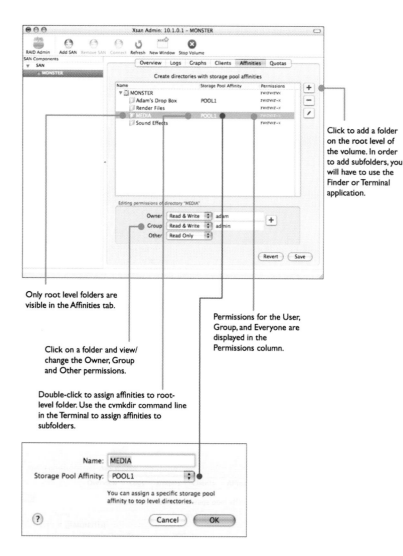

Click to add a folder on the root level of the volume. In order to add subfolders, you will have to use the Finder or Terminal application.

Only root level folders are visible in the Affinities tab.

Click on a folder and view/ change the Owner, Group and Other permissions.

Permissions for the User, Group, and Everyone are displayed in the Permissions column.

Double-click to assign affinities to root-level folder. Use the cvmkdir command line in the Terminal to assign affinities to subfolders.

Setting and Viewing User Quotas

In implementations where the volume will be used by group projects or individual users that require dedicated space, the quotas feature can be used to make sure no user or group goes over a certain storage limit.

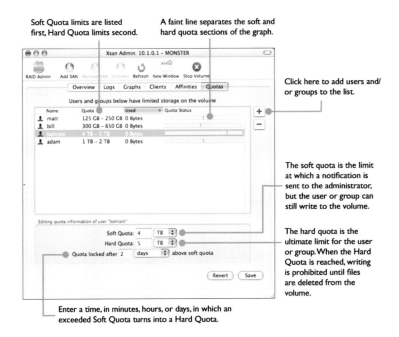

Soft Quota limits are listed first, Hard Quota limits second.

A faint line separates the soft and hard quota sections of the graph.

Click here to add users and/or groups to the list.

The soft quota is the limit at which a notification is sent to the administrator, but the user or group can still write to the volume.

The hard quota is the ultimate limit for the user or group. When the Hard Quota is reached, writing is prohibited until files are deleted from the volume.

Enter a time, in minutes, hours, or days, in which an exceeded Soft Quota turns into a Hard Quota.

Xsan User Quotas can be used by individual SAN users to see where they stand on their storage limits.

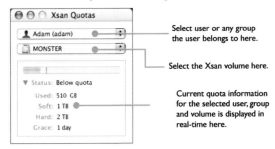

Select user or any group the user belongs to here.

Select the Xsan volume here.

Current quota information for the selected user, group and volume is displayed in real-time here.

Xsan Notifications

Administrators can have major system notifications sent either to email addresses or pagers under this tab. An in-house SMTP server that does not require authentication is needed for this feature of Xsan. In this instance, the notifications machine will need to have access to an external (nonmetadata) network.

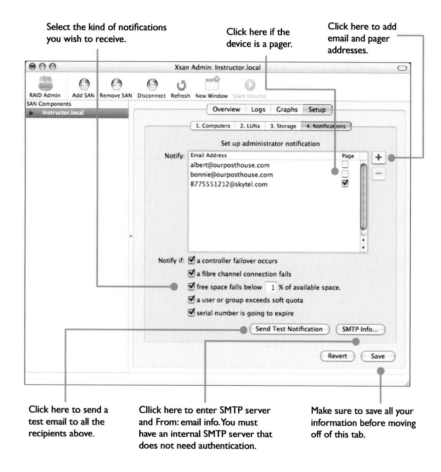

Select the kind of notifications you wish to receive.

Click here if the device is a pager.

Click here to add email and pager addresses.

Click here to send a test email to all the recipients above.

Cllick here to enter SMTP server and From: email info. You must have an internal SMTP server that does not need authentication.

Make sure to save all your information before moving off of this tab.

System and Volume Logs

Click the SAN component to view the system logs of any node attached to the SAN. You can also view any one of the volume logs by clicking the volume name (in this case BIGBOY) and clicking the Logs tab.

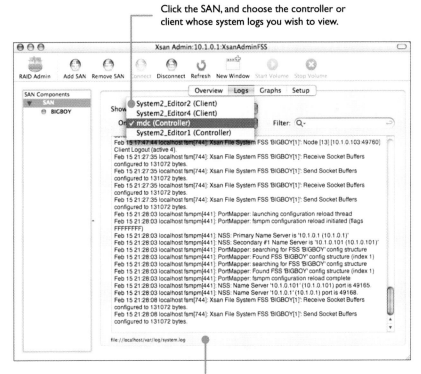

Click the SAN, and choose the controller or client whose system logs you wish to view.

These logs are also available for viewing in the Console Application (Applications > Utilities > Console) of each individual computer.

Xsan Admin Graphs and Statistics

Choose the type of statistics you
would like to see in the graph below.

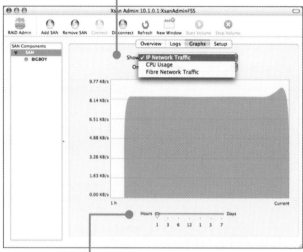

Use the slider to select the graph range –
from I hour to 7 days of statistics.

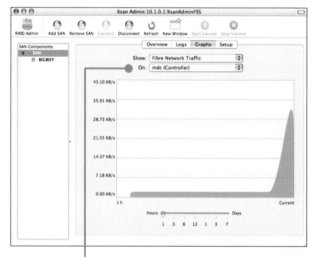

Select the node that you wish to view. In this
example, we are viewing Fibre Channel traffic on
the metadata controller over the past hour.

Xsan Maximums

Parameter	Maximum
Number of computers in a SAN (controllers and clients)	64
Number of storage pools in a volume	512
Number of LUNs in a storage pool	32
Number of LUNs in a volume	512
LUN size	2 TB
Number of files in a volume	4,294,967,296
Volume size	1024 TB
File size	16 TB (Mac OS X v10.3) 1024 TB (Mac OS X v10.4)
Volume name length	70 characters
File or folder name length	251 characters
SAN name length	255 characters
Storage pool name length	255 characters
LUN name (label or disk name)	242 characters

Using the Xsan Tuner Application

You can use Xsan Tuner to test the data and video transfer capabilities of your storage area network and its Xsan volumes. Xsan Tuner can simulate both standard Unix reads and writes and Final Cut Pro video reads and writes for a variety of common video formats. Use Xsan Tuner to see if your SAN can handle planned workloads before you put it into production use.

Note: The Xsan Tuner application will only run on computers running Mac OS X v10.4 or later or Mac OS Server v10.4 or later.

Download the Xsan Tuner application at www.apple.com/support/downloads/.

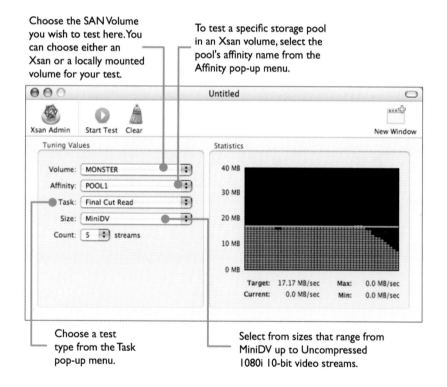

Choose the SAN Volume you wish to test here. You can choose either an Xsan or a locally mounted volume for your test.

To test a specific storage pool in an Xsan volume, select the pool's affinity name from the Affinity pop-up menu.

Choose a test type from the Task pop-up menu.

Select from sizes that range from MiniDV up to Uncompressed 1080i 10-bit video streams.

Using Xsan Controllers with StorNext Clients

You can use ADIC's StorNext software to access an Xsan from a Windows, Unix, AIX, Irix, or Linux computer.

1. Connect the non-Macintosh client to the SAN's Fibre Channel and Ethernet networks.

2. Install the StorNext File System software on the non-Macintosh client following instructions that ADIC provides in the StorNext package.

3. Duplicate the Macintosh Xsan controller's shared secret file on the non-Macintosh client.

   The shared secret file is named .auth_secret.

   On a Macintosh Xsan controller, it is stored in the directory

   /Library/Filesystems/Xsan/config/.

   Copy the file (using the same name) to the non-Macintosh client:

   On SGI IRIX, Sun Solaris, IBM AIX, and Linux StorNext clients, put the file in /usr/cvfs/config.

   On Windows clients, put the file in \%cvfsroot%\config\, where %cvfsroot% is the directory where you installed StorNext.

4. Place a StorNext license file for your non-Macintosh clients on the Macintosh Xsan controller.

   On the Xsan controller, put the file (named license.dat) in the directory /Library/Filesystems/Xsan/config.

   Contact ADIC to obtain a license file for your non-Macintosh clients.

   The non-Macintosh client is ready for use. It should be listed in Xsan Admin, allowing you to mount volumes on it.

Adding Macintosh Clients to a StorNext SAN

If you already have a StorNext file system SAN, you can add a Macintosh client using Xsan.

1. Connect the Macintosh computer to the SAN's Ethernet and Fibre Channel networks.

2. Install the Xsan software on the Macintosh computer.

3. License the Xsan software on the Macintosh client.

   Open Xsan Admin on the client (in Applications/Server) and connect to the local computer. Then select the SAN in the SAN Components list, click Setup, and click Computers. Double-click the client in the list and enter the serial number. (The serial number is on a sticker on the Xsan installer disc sleeve.)

4. Go to an existing StorNext client on the SAN and print a copy of its fsnameservers file.

   On SGI IRIX, Sun Solaris, IBM AIX, and Linux StorNext clients, you can find the file in /usr/cvfs/config.

   On Windows clients, you can find the file in \%cvfsroot%\config\, where %cvfsroot% is the directory in which you installed the StorNext software.

5. Back on the Macintosh client, use a text editor such as vi to create a copy of the fsnameservers file and save it in /Library/Filesystems/Xsan/config/.

6. Force the Xsan software on the Macintosh to read the new fsnameservers file.

   Either restart the Macintosh computer or open the Terminal and type this command:

   ```
   $ sudo kill -HUP `cat /var/run/fsmpm.pid`
   ```

7. Mount the file system.

   If the file system doesn't mount automatically, type this command in Terminal:

   ```
   $ sudo mount -t acfs fsname mountpoint
   ```

   where fsname is the name of the file system, and mountpoint is the location where the file system appears on the Macintosh client (/Volumes/SanVol, for example).

9 Using the Command Line

Although you are perfectly able to configure and set up your SAN without entering the Terminal application, there are times when it will prove invaluable to have a little command-line knowledge under your belt.

Most of the files you will be examining are located in the Xsan folder (/Library/Filesystems/Xsan).

Almost all of the files that you will encounter in the subfolders in the Xsan directory are small XML text files. After you install Xsan Admin, you will notice that the config folder is empty. The config files get pushed to all clients as soon as the metadata controller is set up. Some of the files that are propagated tell the Xsan client which IP address is used to reach the metadata controller and other controllers. There are also config files that tell the host computer which type of node it is, metadata controller or client. Most of these small config files get updated if the admin changes certain properties in the SAN. Since these are only config files, the Xsan Admin application can easily copy these files to all controllers and clients when necessary.

Metadata controllers also have a number of items in their Xsan directory that are absent on client nodes.

- /Library/Filesystems/Xsan/data
- /Library/Filesystems/Xsan/config/<volumename>.cfg
- /Library/Filesystems/Xsan/config/cvlabels
- /Library/Filesystems/Xsan/config/fsmlist

Xsan Directory

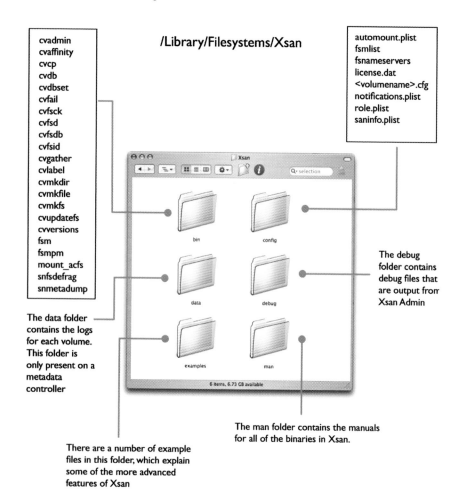

cvadmin
cvaffinity
cvcp
cvdb
cvdbset
cvfail
cvfsck
cvfsd
cvfsdb
cvfsid
cvgather
cvlabel
cvmkdir
cvmkfile
cvmkfs
cvupdatefs
cvversions
fsm
fsmpm
mount_acfs
snfsdefrag
snmetadump

/Library/Filesystems/Xsan

automount.plist
fsmlist
fsnameservers
license.dat
<volumename>.cfg
notifications.plist
role.plist
saninfo.plist

The debug folder contains debug files that are output from Xsan Admin

The data folder contains the logs for each volume. This folder is only present on a metadata controller

The man folder contains the manuals for all of the binaries in Xsan.

There are a number of example files in this folder, which explain some of the more advanced features of Xsan

Using the Shell Commands

To use a command, type the full path. For example:

```
$ sudo /Library/Filesystems/Xsan/bin/cvlabel -l
```

or to change to the directory before typing the command:

```
$ cd /Library/Filesystems/Xsan/bin

$ sudo ./cvlabel -l
```

On Xsan v1.1 and above, it is not necessary to change the path before entering shell commands from Xsan.

Working on Remote Computers

It will be necessary in some of the following examples to run the shell command from the metadata controller. If you are running the Terminal application from a client node, you can SSH into any computer (the metadata controller in this instance) to run the script remotely:

```
$ ssh user@computer
```

where `user` is a user account on the remote computer and `computer` is its Bonjour name, FQDN, or IP address. On a metadata controller with the IP address 10.1.0.1 and admin as the administrator, type:

```
$ ssh admin@10.1.0.1
```

You will then be prompted to enter the password for admin to gain access to this computer.

Remember that remote login on either a server or client must be enabled in order to SSH into that system from another computer. This can be enabled in System Preferences > Sharing.

/LibraryFilesystems/Xsan/bin

cvadmin

cvadmin is an interactive command-line tool. This means that a number of subcommands can be entered after you enter the script. Type quit at the prompt to leave the interactive mode.

Make sure that you have either root access or have entered into the cvadmin interactive mode with sudo cvadmin. If you do not, you will not be able to access the file system. Here's an example of what you see when you enter the interactive mode:

```
mdc:/Library/Filesystems/Xsan/bin admin$ sudo ./cvadmin
Password: ball$$n2
Xsan File System Administrator
Enter command(s)
For command help, enter "help" or "?".
List FSS
File System Services (* indicates service is in control of
FS):
 1>*XSAN[0]              located on localhost:49291 (pid 441)

Select FSM "XSAN"

Created            :    Thu Mar 10 17:11:25 2005
Active Connections :    6
Fs Block Size      :    4K
Msg Buffer Size    :    4K
Disk Devices       :    2
Stripe Groups      :    4
Mirror Groups      :    0
Fs Blocks          :    1073741312 (4.00 TB)
Fs Blocks Free     :    1072583247 (4.00 TB) (99%)

Xsanadmin (XSAN) >
```

`activate [volume|index]`

> Chooses the "active" volume that you want to work with interactively.
>
> `volume` — the name of the volume.
>
> `index` — the numeric ID of the volume (to see a list of these, use the `cvadmin` select command without any parameters).
>
> This command may cause an FSM to activate. If the FSM is already active, no action is taken.

`debug [<value>]`

> Get or Set (with <value>) the FSS debug flags.
>
> Enter `debug` with no value to get current setting and bit meanings. Value should be a valid number. Use `0x` to indicate hexadecimal.

`disable pool [read|write]`

> Prevents read or write access to a storage pool.
>
> `pool` — the name of a storage pool in the currently active volume.

`disks [refresh]`

> Displays ACFS LUNs visible to this machine. If the refresh option is used, the volumes are rescanned. In the following example, two LUNs are visible to the machine.

```
Xsanadmin (XSAN) > disks
Disks (File System XSAN)
ACFS Disk Volumes:
LUN1  on  device:rdisk1    sectors:  4294967295   sector
size: 512
LUN2  on  device:rdisk2    sectors:  4294967295   sector
size: 512
```

`down pool`

> Disallows all access to a storage pool. For example:

```
Xsanadmin (XSAN) > down POOL1
Down Stripe Group "POOL1" (File System "XSAN")
Stripe Group 0 [POOL1]  Status:Down,MetaData,Journal
Total Blocks:1073741312 (4.00 TB)  Free:1072583247 (4.00
TB) (99%)
MultiPath Method:Rotate
Primary  Stripe 0 [POOL1]  Read:Enabled  Write:Enabled
```

`enable pool [read|write]`

> Allows read or write access to a storage pool.

`fail (volume|index)`

> Causes a volume to fail over to a standby controller.

> `volume` — the name of the volume.

> `index` — the numeric ID of the volume (to see a list of these, use the `cvadmin` select command without any parameters).

> If there are no standby controllers available, the volume will fail back to the original metadata controller.

> This command may cause a standby FSM to activate. If the FSM is already active, the FSM will shut down. A standby FSM will take over or the FSM will be relaunched if it is stand-alone.

> In certain instances, you might need to fail a volume to a standby metadata controller (for example, to update the primary metadata controller's software, add RAM, and so on). For example:

```
Xsanadmin (XSAN) > fail XSAN
Fail over FSS "XSAN"
FSS 'XSAN' fail over initiated.
Select FSM "none"
```

`filelocks [yes|no]`

Enables or disables file and record locks. Use the command without any parameter to see the current setting for locks.

`help (?)`

Displays a list and description of all `cvadmin` commands (similar to this section you are reading now).

`multipath pool (rotate|static)`

Specifies how Xsan uses multiple paths to a storage pool. Choose Rotate to have Xsan alternate between the connections for maximum throughput. Choose Static to have Xsan assign each LUN in the storage pool alternately to one of the connections when the volume is mounted.

`paths`

Displays the ACFS disk volumes visible to this machine grouped according to the "controller" identity. For example:

```
Xsanadmin (XSAN) > paths
Paths (File System XSAN)
ACFS Disk Volumes:
Controller: <5000393000006B88>
    LUN1 on device: rdisk1   hba_id: 2 lun: 0 state:
    Available
Controller: <5000393000006CC4>
    LUN2 on device: rdisk2   hba_id: 1 lun: 0 state:
    Available
```

`quit`

Exits from `cvadmin`.

```
quotas [yes|no]
```

> Enables or disables quotas for the active (selected) volume. Use the command without any parameters to see the current setting for quotas.

```
quotas get (user|group) name
```

> Display current quota information for a user or group.
>
> `name` — the name of the user or group.
>
> For example, to check a user named albert or a group named creatives, enter the following:

```
Xsanadmin (XSAN) > quotas get user albert
User:   HL: 3221225472 SL: 2097152 TL: 60 CSZ: 253952
Xsanadmin (XSAN) > quotas get group creatives
Group:   HL: 268435456000 SL: 214748364800 TL: 60 CSZ:
278528
```

> Note the HL (hard limit), SL (soft limit), and TL (time limit) values in the output.

```
quotas set (user|group) name hard soft grace
```

> Set quotas for user or group name.
>
> `name` — the name of the user or group.
> `hard` — hard quota (bytes).
> `soft` — soft quota (bytes).
> `grace` — grace period (minutes).

```
quotacheck
```

> Recalculates the amount of space consumed (the current size field of the quota record) by all users and groups in the file system. This command can be run on an active file system, although file updates (writes, truncates, and so on) will be delayed until `quotacheck` is completed.

`repquota`

Generates quota reports for all users and groups in the file system. These files will be saved in /Library/Filesystems/Xsan/data/ <volume>.

`quota_report.txt` — text file.

quota_report.csv — comma-delimited file.

quota_regen.in — `cvadmin` commands that will set up identical quotas on another controller. You can use `cvadmin` `-f` to execute these commands.

`repof`

Creates a report of open files on the active volume in the file / Library/Filesystems/Xsan/data/<volume>/open_file_report.txt.

`select [volume]`

Chooses the "active" volume that you want to work with. The name of the currently active volume appears following the command prompt in interactive mode.

For example: `Xsanadmin (Vol1) >`. To see a list of running volumes, leave off the volume parameter.

`volume` — the name of an Xsan volume.

```
show [ <pool> ] [ long ]
```

Shows all pools or a specific pool `<pool>`. Adding the modifier `long` shows more verbose information. For example:

```
Xsanadmin (XSAN) > show POOL1 long
Show stripe group "POOL1" (File System "XSAN")
Stripe Group 0 [POOL1]   Status:Up,MetaData,Journal
    Total Blocks:1073741312 (4.00 TB)   Free:1072583247
    (4.00 TB) (99%)
    MultiPath Method:Rotate
    Stripe Depth:2   Stripe Breadth:256 blocks (1024.00
    KB)
    Affinity Key:POOL1
    Realtime limit IO/sec:0  (~0 mb/sec)  Non-Realtime
    reserve IO/sec:0
        Committed RTIO/sec:0 Non-RTIO clients:0 Non-RTIO
        hint IO/sec:0
    Disk stripes:
        Primary  Stripe 0 [POOL1]  Read:Enabled  Write:
        Enabled
            Node 0 [LUN1]
            Node 1 [LUN2]
```

```
start volume [on] [controller]
```

Starts the volume based on the information in its configuration file (/Library/Filesystems/Xsan/config/volume.cfg).

`controller` — The address of the controller on which to start the volume's FSM process.

```
stat
```

Displays information about the active volume. For example:

```
Xsanadmin (XSAN) > stat
Stat (File System "XSAN")

Created              :    Thu Mar 10 17:11:25 2005
Active Connections   :    4
Fs Block Size        :    4K
Msg Buffer Size      :    4K
Disk Devices         :    2
Stripe Groups        :    1
Mirror Groups        :    0
Fs Blocks            :    1073741312 (4.00 TB)
Fs Blocks Free       :    1072583247 (4.00 TB) (99%)
```

```
stop <volume> | <index_number>
```

Stops the FSM processes for `<volume>` or `<index_number>`. Stopping by name will stop all instances of `<volume>`. Stopping by number stops only the service associated with the index. Indexes are displayed on the left side as "nn>" when using the `select` command.

```
up pool
```

Allows access to the specified storage pool. For example:

```
Xsanadmin (XSAN) > up POOL1
Up Stripe Group "POOL1" (File System "XSAN")
Stripe Group 0 [POOL1]  Status:Up,MetaData,Journal
Total Blocks:1073741312 (4.00 TB)  Free:1072583247 (4.00
TB) (99%)
MultiPath Method:Rotate
Primary  Stripe 0 [POOL1]  Read:Enabled  Write:Enabled
```

who

Displays client information for the active volume.

```
Xsanadmin (XSAN) > who
Who (File System "XSAN")
#    ACFS   I.D.   Type  Location     Up Time     License Expires
--   --------- ---- ----------- ------- --------------
0>              FSM                0d 2h 26m   N/A
2>              CLI   10.1.0.103   0d 2h 24m   N/A
7>              CLI   10.1.0.104   0d 2h 24m   N/A
9>              CLI   10.1.0.105   0d 2h 24m   N/A
10>             CLI   10.1.0.106   0d 2h 24m   N/A
15>             CLI   localhost    0d 0h 30m   N/A
54>             ADM   localhost    0d 0h 1m    N/A
```

cvaffinity

Establishes an affinity to a storage pool or lists a files current affinity.

For example, to set an affinity for the folder Render Files to the storage pool POOL1, type the following:

```
mdc:/Library/Filesystems/Xsan/bin  root#  ./cvaffinity  -k
POOL1 /Volumes/XSAN/MEDIA/albert/Render\ Files/
```

To check a folder's affinity:

```
mdc:/Library/Filesystems/Xsan/bin  root#  ./cvaffinity  -l  /
Volumes/XSAN/Media
```

```
/Volumes/XSAN/Media: POOL1 (0x524f53434f520000)
```

cvcp

Performs high-speed file copies to or from an Xsan volume. You can use this command to

- Copy files or directories
- Copy tar-formatted data to a directory
- Copy a file or directory to a tar-formatted data stream

```
$ cvcp [options] source destination
```

Example: Copy the file lightning to /Volumes/Xsan/Media:

```
$ cvcp lightning /Volumes/Xsan/Media
```

Check the manual pages (man cvcp) to view additional options for this command.

cvdb

Provides a mechanism for developers and system administrators to extract debugging information from the Xsan File System (Xsan) client files system. It can also be used by system administrators to change the level of system logging that the client file system performs.

cvdbset

A tool for system administrators to control cvdb tracing information from the Xsan File System (Xsan) client file system. The main purpose of this command is to facilitate the restriction of client tracing to a certain set of modules.

cvfsck

Checks and repairs Xsan file system metadata corruption due to a system crash, bad disk, or other catastrophic failure. This program also can list all of the existing files and their pertinent statistics, such as inode number, size, file type, and location in the volume. If the volume is active, it may be checked only in a read-only mode. In this mode, modifications are noted, but not committed. The -n option may be used to perform a read-only check as well.

The file-system-checking program must be run on the machine where the File System Services are running. cvfsck reads the configuration file and compares the configuration against the metadata it finds. If there are discrepancies with the configuration, the volume is repaired to reflect the correct configuration.

```
$ cvfsck [options] volume
```

Check the manual pages (man cvfsck) to view additional options for this command.

cvfsd

cvfsd is a server daemon that is launched by the Xsan File System mount_cvfs(1M) command. It is an internal kernel thread and is used for network communication to the File System Manager. Multiple cvfsd threads are launched for each Xsan volume.

cvgather

The `cvgather` program is used to collect debug information from a volume. This creates a tar file of the system's Xsan File System debug logs, configuration, version information, and disk devices. The program will collect client debug information on client machines and server information on server machines, as well as portmap information from all machines. System log files as well as Xsan log files are included. At the users option, `cvgather` also collects core files from user space utilities, such as the FSM, and also from the operating system kernel, when available. This information provides Apple technical support staff with enough information to deal with most problems encountered by Xsan users.

For example:

```
mdc:/Library/Filesystems/Xsan/bin root# ./cvgather -f XSAN
  ./cvgather: uname -a
  ./cvgather: /Library/Filesystems/Xsan/bin/cvversions
  ./cvgather: /Library/Filesystems/Xsan/bin/cvlabel -c
  ./cvgather: /Library/Filesystems/Xsan/bin/cvfsid
  ./cvgather: /var/log/system.log
  ./cvgather: /Library/Filesystems/Xsan/config/XSAN.cfg
  ./cvgather: /Library/Filesystems/Xsan/config/fsnameservers
  ./cvgather: /Library/Filesystems/Xsan/config/fsmlist
  ./cvgather: /Library/Filesystems/Xsan/debug/nssdbg.out
  ./cvgather: /Library/Filesystems/Xsan/debug/cvfsd.out
  ./cvgather: /Library/Filesystems/Xsan/debug/fsmpm.out
  ./cvgather: /Library/Filesystems/Xsan/data/XSAN/log/cvlog
Creating tar ball.
Wrote 110592 bytes to /Library/Filesystems/Xsan/bin/MacOSX_mdc.
local_XSAN.tgz
  ./cvgather: Complete.
```

The new file it creates in the /Library/Filesystems/Xsan/bin directory can be emailed to an AppleCare specialist for further diagnostic of your system.

cvlabel

Initializes LUNs so they can be added to storage pools. The unlabel option is necessary when attempting to connect a RAID formatted for Xsan and use it as a direct-attached storage device. LUNs must be unlabeled in order to be initialized as HFS+ volumes in Disk Utility.

For example, to view labeled LUNs:

```
mdc:/Library/Filesystems/Xsan/bin root# ./cvlabel -l

/dev/rdisk1 [APPLE    Xserve  RAID      1.26]  CVFS  "LUN1"
Sectors:  4294967295.  SectorSize:  512.  Maximum  sectors:
4680626944.

/dev/rdisk2 [APPLE    Xserve  RAID      1.26]  CVFS  "LUN2"
Sectors:  4294967295.  SectorSize:  512.  Maximum  sectors:
4680626944.
```

To unlabel LUNs:

```
mdc:/Library/Filesystems/Xsan/bin root# ./cvlabel -u LUN2


*WARNING* This program will remove the volume label from the
device specified (LUN2).

After execution, the devices will not be usable by the Xsan
File System. You will have to relabel the device to use it
on the Xsan File System.



Do you want to proceed? (Y / N ) -> Y
```

cvmkdir

You can use Xsan Admin to assign an affinity to a folder at the top level of a volume, but to assign an affinity to a folder that is inside another folder you need to use the `cvmkdir` command-line tool.

For example, to assign an affinity for the storage pool POOL1 to folder Audio which is inside the folder Projects on the volume BIGBOY, you would type the following:

```
$ sudo ./cvmkdir -k POOL1 /Volumes/BIGBOY/projects/audio
```

cvmkfile

Allocated space for a file on a Xsan volume.

For example, to allocate 2 GB of space for the file dafney on the storage pool POOL1:

```
$ cvmkfile -k POOL1 2g dafney
```

Check the manual pages (`man cvmkfile`) to view additional options for this command.

cvmkfs

Initializes an Xsan volume based on the information in the corresponding configuration file for the volume in /Library/Filesystems/Xsan/config/<vol>.cfg)

WARNING—Initializing a volume destroys all existing data on the volume.

cvupdatefs

Applies configuration file changes to a volume after you modify the volume's configuration files. The volume will have to be stopped in order to run this script.

```
$ cvupdatefs volume
```

In the following example, POOL1's journal will be resized. This is because the volume's configuration file was changed (/Library/Filesystems/Xsan/config/<volume>.cfg), and the cvupdatefs script was run.

```
mdc:/Library/Filesystems/Xsan/bin root# ./cvupdatefs
Xsan File System File Systems on host mdc.local:

1)  XSAN

Choose a file system by number (1-1) or zero (0) to exit -
> 1

The following changes have been detected in the configura-
tion
Please review these changes carefully.

Stripe Group Name  Stripe Status  MetaData   Journal
=================  =============  ========   =======
POOL1              No Change      No Change  Resize

This will modify the file system "XSAN".
Are you sure you want to continue? [y/N] y
Flushing journal entries...  done
Freeing old journal space...
Allocating new journal space...
Updating ICB information...
Updating SuperBlock information...
File system 'XSAN' was modified.
```

cvversions

Displays Xsan volume and client information. Useful when checking to see if the server and client software match.

```
mdc:/Library/Filesystems/Xsan/bin root# ./cvversions

File System Server:
  Server Revision 2.6.1 Build 16
  Built for Darwin 8.0
  Created on Fri Aug 12 14:23:18 PDT 2005
  Server Revision 2.6.1 Build 16

File System Client:
  Client Revision 2.6.1 Build 16
  Built for Darwin 8.0
  Created on Fri Aug 12 14:26:25 PDT 2005
  Built in /SourceCache/XsanFS/XsanFS-261.16
```

mount_acfs

A mount helper utility that mounts an Xsan volume on client machines.

```
$ sudo mount -t acfs volume mountpoint
```

snfs_defrag

Defragments a file by reallocating its data in a single extent. This can improve read and write performance for a file by increasing disk efficiency and reducing file metadata management overhead.

For example, to defrag the entire volume BIGBOY, use the -r option:

```
mdc:/Library/Filesystems/Xsan/bin root# ./snfsdefrag -r /
Volumes/BIGBOY/

28 files visited: 2 defragged, 26 skipped
```

10 Troubleshooting

Xsan will not mount any volume that has the same name as any existing volume or folder located at /Volumes/.

Unlike some mounting mechanisms that automatically resolve name conflicts (for example, the Finder appends characters to each mounted volume name), the Xsan backend agent simply won't mount the volumes.

To avoid this issue, create a unique name for each volume to be mounted.

An Xsan volume can't be renamed in the Finder.

You can't change the name of a mounted Xsan volume via the Finder. If you try, you get a message saying the name you've typed cannot be used, even if it is an acceptable Xsan volume name.

To rename an Xsan volume, you must use Xsan Admin to reinitialize the volume.

Mismatched optical transceivers (GBICs) can cause Fibre Channel communication errors and degrade SAN performance.

To ensure good performance, use identical transceivers (same manufacturer and model number) on both ends of your Fibre Channel cables.

cvadmin cannot list FSS.

If you get the response "Cannot list FSS - reason -Bad file descriptor" when you run the `cvadmin` tool, make sure you are using the tool as the root user. Either log in as the root user or use the `sudo` command to run the tool. For example:

```
$ sudo ./cvadmin
```

After updating to 10.3.8, Xsan is disabled.

If you're running Xsan and just installed Security Update 2005-002, you may come across an issue where the Xsan file system becomes disabled and won't start up. This happens because this security update overwrites the hostconfig file in the /etc directory, which removes the command to start the Xsan file system. To resolve this issue, modify the hostconfig file as follows:

1. Launch the Terminal (choose Applications > Utilities).

2. Change to the root user by typing su root. Type your password when prompted.

3. Type cd /etc to navigate to the /etc directory.

4. Open your preferred editor (such as vi, emacs, or pico), and use it to add the following line to the bottom of the hostconfig file:

   `ACFS=-YES-.`

5. Save the file and then close your editor application.

6. Restart your computer.

   Note: You will need to modify the hostconfig file on all Xsan clients and metadata controllers after installing Security Update 2005-002.

   Make sure `ACFS=YES` in the hostconfig file is on the metadata controller as well.

Estimating metadata storage requirements

To estimate the amount of space required for Xsan volume metadata, you can assume that 10 million files on a volume will require roughly 10 GB of metadata on the volume's metadata storage pool.

LUNs can't be added to metadata and journaling storage pools.

You can't add LUNs to a storage pool that is already being used to store journal data or metadata. This applies to any storage pool set to be used for "Journaling and metadata only" or "Any data."

If you try to drag a LUN to a metadata or journaling storage pool, no insertion point appears.

To check the data types a storage pool is used for, perform the following steps:

1. Open Xsan Admin, select the SAN or controller, and click Setup.

2. Click Storage, then double-click the storage pool in the list. Look next to "Use for" in the storage pool settings sheet to see how the storage pool is used.

Xsan Admin lists duplicate LUNs.

If you are using mismatched versions of Xserve RAID firmware and the RAID Admin application, you might see duplicate LUNs listed in the LUNs pane in Xsan Admin.

To remove duplicate LUNs, perform the following step:

1. Open RAID Admin, select the Xserve RAID system that is hosting the LUNs, and choose System > Repair LUN Map.

   If you don't see the Repair LUN Map option, upgrade to the latest version of RAID Admin (available at www.apple.com/support). To avoid this problem in the future, always use the latest version of RAID Admin and use it to install the latest firmware on your Xserve RAID systems.

Store metadata on first or second storage pool.

To avoid file system configuration problems, store volume metadata on only the first or second storage pool in a volume (the first two storage pools listed under the volume in the Storage pane of Xsan Admin).

Otherwise, your controllers might fail over and you might see messages saying "A server you are using is no longer available" when a controller restarts.

To see if a storage pool is used for metadata, perform the following steps:

1. Open Xsan Admin, select the SAN or controller, and click Setup.

2. Click Storage, then double-click the storage pool in the list. Look next to "Use for" in the storage pool settings sheet. If either "Any data" or "Journaling and metadata only" is selected, metadata is stored on the storage pool.

Assigning affinities to subfolders on the SAN

The `cvmkdir` command allows you to assign an affinity to a directory by typing the following:

```
$ sudo cvaffinity -k pool path
```

The instructions in the Xsan Administrator's Guide say you can use the storage pool name for the `<affinity>` parameter. This is true only if the storage pool name is eight characters or less, in which case the storage pool name and the affinity name are the same. If the storage pool name is longer than eight characters, the affinity name is an eight-character name that Xsan creates based on the storage pool name, and you need to use this shorter affinity name for the `<affinity>` parameter. This storage pool name can be found in the configuration file for the volume located in /Library/Filesystems/Xsan/config/<volume>.cfg.

Upgrading Xsan controller software

If your configuration includes a standby controller, you can upgrade the Xsan software without interrupting the SAN. Xsan controller software is always compatible with the preceding version of the client software. (Controllers can be one version ahead of clients.) So, you can upgrade your controllers first, and your client computers will continue to work until it is convenient to upgrade them to the same version.

1. To switch all volumes to a standby controller, go to the primary controller, open Terminal, and type:

```
$ cd /Library/Filesystems/Xsan/bin

$ sudo ./cvadmin fail <volume>
```

where `<volume>` is the name of an Xsan volume.

To see a list of volumes hosted by the controller, type:

```
$ sudo ./cvadmin select
```

To see which controller is hosting a volume:

Open Xsan Admin, select the volume, and click Overview.

2. When all volumes are being hosted by the standby controller, upgrade the software on the primary controller.

3. When you are finished upgrading the primary controller, use the methods in step 1 to switch control of the active volumes back to the primary controller.

Now you can upgrade the standby controller.

After slicing, some LUNs aren't listed in Xsan Admin.

If you slice an array that was previously labeled for use with Xsan, you might need to remove the old label from the first slice.

To see if the LUN is mounted using its old label, open Terminal and type the following:

```
$ sudo cvlabel -l -s
```

(The `cvlabel` tool is in /Library/Filesystems/xsan/bin.)

This will show the old label. In the following sample output, the label is sanvol1.

```
/dev/rdisk4/ [APPLE Xserve RAID 1.20] CVFS "sanvol1"
```

To remove the old label, type the following:

```
$ sudo cvlabel -u <label>
```

where `<label>` is the old label (`sanvol1` in the example).

After you unlabel the LUN, it should appear in the LUNs pane in Xsan Admin.

LUN doesn't have as much free space as expected.

To make striping across LUNs possible, Xsan automatically adjusts LUN sizes to make all LUNs in a storage pool the same size as the smallest LUN in the pool. Xsan doesn't use the extra space on larger LUNs when you mix LUNs of different sizes in the same storage pool.

Can't connect to a SAN computer from Xsan Admin

If there is a firewall between the admin computer and the SAN computer, make sure TCP port 311 is open.

User sees error code –1425 in finder when copying files to the SAN.

The user is trying to occupy more space than allowed by his or her hard quota.

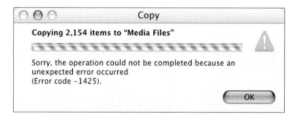

New folders may have unexpected group ownership

When creating folders on an Xsan volume, the group owner of a new folder is the primary group of the user who created it—not the group owner of the parent folder.

Because of this, users who are members of a common group, but who have other primary groups, may create folders with varying ownership inside the folder of their common group. Members of this group may expect to have access to everything inside the common group's folder, but that won't be the case.

To resolve the issue, log in as an administrator, select the affected folder, and Get Info. In the Ownership & Permissions section of the Info window, change the ownership to the desired group.

New files and folders have read-only group ownership.

When creating a new file or folder on the SAN, you will notice that the group permissions are set to "read only." This is due to the umask settings on the client computer. In order to change the setting so that file and folder creation allows the group to have read and write access, use the Terminal to alter the umask.

In the Terminal, a per-user umask can be changed easily by typing the following:

```
$ defaults write -g NSUmask -int 2
```

The above setting of 002 means that any new files or folders will have their group permissions set to "Read & Write."

There are also third-party software applications available that will globally update the umask so that you don't have to enter the Terminal.

Don't use mv command to move files to non-Xsan volumes.

If you want to move files from an Xsan volume to a non-Xsan volume using the command line, don't use the `mv` command. Instead, use the `cp` command to copy the files and then delete the originals from the Xsan volume.

Can't see storage via Fibre Channel connection

Some Fibre Channel switches can suppress the generation of Registered State Change Notification (RSCN) messages on a port basis. This setting allows storage devices to inform hosts that it has entered the network. In some cases, if an Xsan client is restarted, a slight pause may occur throughout the entire Fibre network. This is unwanted in a video environment since it may cause dropped frames or other unexpected behavior. This suppression should be enabled only on ports connected to initiators (CPUs) and not targets (Xserve RAIDs).

On Emulex switches, target ports should be set to "Targets with Stealth," and initiators should be set to "Initiators with Stealth."

Troubleshooting

On QLogic switches, RSCN is disabled by enabling a feature known as I/O Stream Guard. In the following image, notice that the target port (14) is selected, and the I/O Stream Guard option is disabled. On initiator ports, also remember to disable Device Scan.

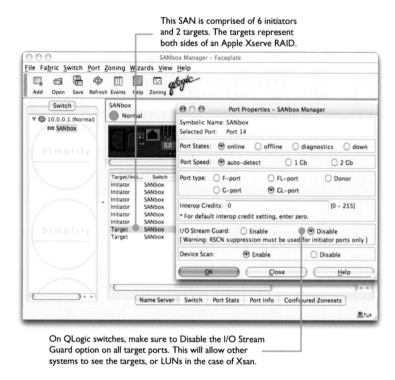

This SAN is comprised of 6 initiators and 2 targets. The targets represent both sides of an Apple Xserve RAID.

On QLogic switches, make sure to Disable the I/O Stream Guard option on all target ports. This will allow other systems to see the targets, or LUNs in the case of Xsan.

QLogic-SANbox Manager

For Xserve RAID controllers, choose Target with Stealth. This setting allows storage devices to inform hosts that it has entered the network.

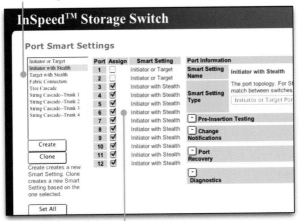

Choose Initiator with Stealth for all initiator ports (Xsan clients). This setting allows host devices to be made aware when new storage devices are available.

Emulex-Web Manager

11 Glossary

affinity

An association (affinity) between a folder on an Xsan volume and one of the pools that make up the volume. The affinity guarantees that files that users place in the folder are stored only on the pools that have been formatted to meet specific capacity, performance, and reliability goals.

AFP (Apple Filing Protocol)

A network file system protocol used to share files and network services. AFP uses TCP/IP and other protocols to communicate between systems on a network.

arbitrated loop

This term may arise when planning a storage area network (SAN), as the customer may want to save money by deploying a Fibre Channel hub rather than a Fibre Channel switch. The internal wiring of the hub has all the ports connected as a physical loop and uses a special protocol that defines how the connected systems gain control of the loop to communicate with other devices connected to the hub. Note that in an arbitrated loop, the bandwidth is shared among all of the systems and devices. So if system 1 has 200 GB of data to transmit, and system 2 has 350 GB to transmit, and the hub supports 100 GB/s, they arbitrate with each other to obtain control of the 100 GB/s hub and may end up with each one having a certain number of usage spots to transmit 100 GB at a time.

autoloader

A tape backup system that uses a robotic mechanism to automatically load and unload cartridges into a tape drive. When combined with a software solution for hierarchical storage management or information lifecycle management, users may not even be aware that the file is being retrieved from or stored to tape. Autoloaders can also be used to provide unattended data backup and file restoration.

availability

For users with high-reliability requirements solutions or downtime/uptime requirements, availability is a metric they may specify for their solution (see also MTBF). Typically, the number is based on the amount of time that a system is available during those periods when it is expected to be available (for example, excluding scheduled backups). Availability is often measured as a percentage of an elapsed year. For example, 99.95 percent availability equates to 4.38 hours of downtime in a year (0.0005 x 365 x 24 = 4.38) for a system that is expected to be available all the time. This is a key measurement for mission-critical systems. Providing the highest level of availability (99.999 percent) usually requires redundant servers and access to shared storage such as an Xsan solution provides.

bandwidth

Bandwidth (synonymous with data transfer rate) is used to describe the amount of data that can be transferred through a system or network connection in a given time period. Different connection types (Ethernet, Fibre Channel, FireWire) and the protocols supported (TCP/IP and SCSI, for example) on those connection types will dictate the maximum potential data rate. The rate is usually indicated in bits or bytes per second. It is important to assess bandwidth requirements when deploying solutions such as Web servers, network-based storage, and creative workflow applications, to ensure bandwidth to the storage will meet the requirements. For example, a video-streaming deployment will need high-bandwidth networking solutions between the storage and servers to ensure an adequate frame rate. The number of simultaneous streams will need to be assessed to determine the specific network topology.

block

Storage devices contain disks that are divided into tracks and then into sectors. When the disk is formatted, it can be optimized for performance by specifying the number of sectors the operating system can read from (or write to) the disk at a time. This setting is the block factor. By default, a sector of data is typically 512 bytes. The application that the storage will be used for, however, may support larger block sizes for faster performance. Video and database deployments, for example, should include a step to determine the block size needed to sustain the desired I/O.

cache

This refers to special-purpose memory on a server or storage device used to increase performance. Storage cache usually resides on RAID controllers and boosts performance because the CPU doesn't have to wait for a disk head to spin. Data can be written to and read directly from cache. For example, cache can be used to store data fetched from a disk, which is particularly useful if it is data that may be accessed frequently, or by multiple applications or multiple users. Some solutions support prefetching algorithms that essentially guess and fetch anticipated data from disk, based on the original data request. This also decreases wait time. Ideally, the cache size is a multiple of the block size so the operating system can retrieve complete data blocks.

cascading

This refers to deploying switches in a tiered manner to increase the number of simultaneous connections to a server or storage device. This enables reliability and scalability in a network/storage fabric. It is critical to plan this carefully to ensure the desired I/O performance is maintained. For example, an Xserve RAID has two Fibre Channel ports. Each of those ports can be connected to a Fibre Channel switch that may have 16 ports, which would allow 16 connections to the Xserve RAID. If more connections were needed (which may be in an Xsan configuration), then that first switch can connect to up to 16 more switches. Note, however, that the more simultaneous connections are enabled, the greater the potential is for slower performance. For example, the scenario just outlined could enable 256 servers retrieving data from one Xserve RAID, which may be suitable for some transactions, but not for something like video streaming. Some manufacturers refer to this as inter-switch linking or trunking.

client

For the licensing of Xsan, a client is the system directly attached to the SAN via a Fibre Channel connection. Clients can also refer to a system on a network that receives network services from a server, such as client systems connecting to a file or print server. It can also refer to a software program that requests services from other programs or servers. Pay careful attention to the context. For example, someone might describe user systems as clients that can attach to file servers, and those servers in turn may be clients to a SAN file system. It is important to interpret the context as this becomes important when you are discussing licensing costs and planning deployments.

cluster file system

Cluster file systems allow multiple systems to simultaneously access the same storage. This differs from a traditional file system like HFS+, which can be shared only by using network protocols like NFS, AFP, and SMB. Xsan and other SAN file systems are sometimes referred to as cluster file systems.

DAS (direct-attached storage)

Refers to disks inside a system or directly attached as through a SCSI, FireWire, USB, or Fibre Channel interface. For example, when Xserve RAID is connected to the Fibre Channel PCI card interface in a server or workstation, the RAID is "direct attached" to that server or workstation. DAS is generally considered very fast since the storage can be accessed at block I/O rates. It can also be shared with other computers using a network sharing protocol, such as AFP, SMB, CIFS, or NFS, but this is at file I/O rates. Xsan solves this performance issue by allowing multiple systems to access the same volumes and files, concurrently, at block I/O rates over a Fibre Channel network.

directory services

A mechanism of managing information about users, groups of users, and equipment. Organizing this information in a centralized database allows administrators to set up relationships between people and resources in one place, rather than controlling access by configuring each user's system. Active Directory and Open Directory are examples. Xsan can use directory services to enable features such as user storage quotas.

DNS (domain name service)

A software service that enables translation of domain names (for example, www.apple.com) into an IP address. Servers with DNS are generally available from Internet service providers to support their users accessing Web sites with names instead of IP addresses. Within a company, a network system administrator may also choose to enable DNS (available with Mac OS X Server) to support fast identification of hosts within the private network or SAN.

ECC RAM (error correcting code)

This type of RAM is used in Xserve G5 CPUs. ECC RAM can detect errors (both single- and multibit) and is able to fix single-bit errors on the fly. This is transparent to the user and is extremely useful in systems that are kept online constantly, such as Xsan metadata controllers.

fabric

In a storage area network, with or without a cluster file system like Xsan, the fabric is the collective term for the Fibre Channel HBAs, switches, and cables that connect the servers and storage devices. A SAN installation may contain multiple fabrics for redundancy or scalability.

failover

A strategy associated with high-availability deployments. A failover configuration increases the reliability of a server or storage solution. Generally, a failover configuration includes two or more systems configured identically but with monitoring between them. For example, a pair of servers configured with failover (the high- and medium-priority controllers) will have a primary server that responds to metadata network requests, and a secondary, identical server that monitors the status of the primary server. The secondary server services requests only when the primary server becomes unavailable.

Failover may also be mentioned in the context of storage solutions. In this case, the high-availability and reliability points a customer may want to discuss include redundancy of RAID controllers and mirrored RAID sets.

Fibre Channel switch (Fabric Switch)

Used to create a high-performance Fibre Channel network, a switch enables multiple connections between servers and storage at full (rather than shared) Fibre Channel bandwidth. So if server 1 needs to transmit 200 GB, and server 2 needs to transmit 350 GB, and the switch supports 100 GB/s, then both servers get a connection of 100 GB/s.

headless system

A system that does not have a display attached. An Xserve G5, for example, does not need a graphics display and can be administered either remotely using the administration software included or from the command line using SSH. In cases where an administrator wants to log in, the operating system creates a virtual frame buffer that allows applications to be displayed remotely on other systems, or displays an entire virtual desktop (as when being accessed through Apple Remote Desktop).

HBA (host bus adapter)

The interface on a storage device, a server, or workstation used to convert outbound block data to packets suitable for transport over the applicable format of the adapter (for example, FireWire, SCSI, Fibre Channel) and to convert inbound packets to block data. Xsan requires Fibre Channel HBAs in order for the Xsan Admin program to recognize storage.

hot spare

This refers to a drive in a RAID configuration that is unused but allocated to be available if a drive in a RAID-1 or RAID-5 configuration fails. The hot spare will assume the role of the failed drive, and the data will be automatically rebuilt. This is a deployment design strategy and is applicable for users with high-reliability and high-availability needs.

iSCSI

A newer storage networking protocol that attempts to transmit blocks of data more effectively over IP (as for Ethernet) than NFS, for example. iSCSI is still limited by issues described in file I/O, although it attempts to approach block VO performance. Users may ask for a comparison of Xsan to an iSCSI solution. These are not really comparable. An Xsan solution provides much more than any iSCSI solution could, including performance.

LDAP

An industry-standard protocol used in directory service tools (Microsoft's Active Directory, Novell's eDirectory, Apple's Open Directory) to locate organizations, individuals, and other resources such as files and devices (for example Cisco supports LDAP for identification of its devices) in a network. By using an industry-standard protocol, vendors are able to offer more seamless integration with heterogeneous environments.

LUN (logical unit number)

A LUN may be a disk, a RAID set, or a slice of a RAID set. Xserve RAIDs can be subdivided into many LUNs. A LUN will typically be formatted with a specific RAID strategy to achieve performance or data redundancy goals. Even though access can be assigned to a LUN, and this seems to be the same as access to a volume, a LUN and a volume are different. A LUN is basically the address of a physical disk, and while this address can be used for access control, this is a manual strategy that is less often used as it can be somewhat less flexible in capacity management. In contrast, a volume can consist of multiple LUNs.

metadata controller

This software component of a SAN file system manages access to files on the volumes that are part of the SAN file system. Client systems send file requests to the metadata controller, which determines whether the requesting system has permission, and if so, whether the file is already being used for read or write, then grants an access token along with the file location. The requesting system can then access the file. The metadata controller typically resides on a system that is used for no other purpose and communicates to all client systems over a private Ethernet network.

mirroring

A storage strategy used for high-availability, redundancy, and disaster-recovery planning, in which data is written to more than one location, generally at the same time. Mirroring can be set up within a single RAID array by formatting the array with RAID level, or an entire rack of RAID arrays can be mirrored by point-in-time copying to another identically configured rack of arrays.

multipathing

The utilization of both paths (two) between the Fibre Channel ports of a system and the Fibre Channel switch(es) to the storage. When both paths are connected to the same switch, the system will automatically utilize both of them for either high availability or to increase bandwidth. If they are connected to separate switches, the system will utilize them only for high availability. The system will automatically determine which utilization model is most appropriate. If both paths are connected to one switch, then their combined bandwidth will be used for greater throughput. In either configuration, if one path becomes unavailable, the system will automatically fail over all data traffic to the remaining path (high availability).

NAS (network-attached storage)

A general term for stand-alone storage devices connected directly to a local area network (LAN) or a wide area network (WAN) for easy access by multiple servers, multiple operating systems, or multiple clients. These devices typically don't include a full operating system; rather they have a special-purpose operating system designed to handle only specific data read, write, and sharing functions.

NAT (Network Address Translation)

This is a service usually offered on a router, a network device that translates computer addresses between networks, but is also included with Mac OS X Server. NAT is used to convert a public Internet address (as used on the Internet) to an internal network address. This process allows a single unique IP address to represent an entire group of computers to anything outside their network The benefits are increased security since the private network addresses are not shared outside the company, and a reduction in the number of Internet addresses that a company will need.

NFS (Network File System)

A file sharing protocol used on Unix and Linux systems. NFS allows users to access shared folders over Ethernet (TCP/IP).

node

This term is used to refer to a device on a network, such as direct clients of an Xsan storage area network.

partition

Refers to the division of a disk drive into more than one logical unit. This allows a number of activities, such as different operating systems being installed (and booted from); sizing of the disk to match specific operating system requirements; and isolating data storage from the operating system drive to help minimize data corruption. Partitioning is usually done on a laptop, workstation, or perhaps on a server with a single disk.

RAID (redundant array of independent disks)

A collection (array) of disk drives housed in a single chassis that allows management of the array in ways that support requirements for increased data integrity, fault tolerance, and performance. The drives may be configured into one or more LUNs, and collections of LUNs from that array or from multiple arrays can be grouped as volumes.

RAID controllers

Integrated within the RAID array chassis, RAID controllers handle I/O requests (translate the file request into a block location, retrieve it, and vice versa), monitor the status of drives and other array components, and have specialized processors to manage data writes according to the RAID level specified during the formatting of the array.

replication

Refers to the duplication of data (usually a database) to another site, as for backup or access from multiple sites. For example, directory services can be replicated to multiple geographic locations to increase performance for users accessing the data remotely. On a scheduled basis, data is pushed from the master server to the replication servers. Typically only changes are pushed, rather than an entire database.

Samba

A freeware file-sharing solution based on SMB/CIFS that allows UNIX, Linux, IRIX, Mac OS, and other operating systems to provide file or print services to Windows clients or servers.

SMB/CIFS (Server Message Block / Common Internet File System)

A protocol developed by Microsoft for Windows systems, SMB enabled client systems to access network resources such as shared files, printers, and so on. Leveraging an open-source version of SMB, the Internet Engineering Task Force developed a complementary protocol (CIFS) to support Web applications that need more flexible file exchange than offered by FTP.

zoning

An access control mechanism similar to LUN masking, zoning is a manual method to create logical groups in a SAN. Devices attached to the Fibre Channel fabric of a SAN may be grouped into zones based on their LUN number, host name, physical device ID (for example WWN), port number, and so on. Devices in the same zone have visibility and access to each other; devices located in different zones do not.

Index

Index

viewing using RAID Admin, 44
audio pool
  configuring three or more RAIDs, 36-37
  configuring two or more RAIDs, 34-35
authentication
  in basic Xsan topology example, 16
  groups and, 73
  local, 61, 69
autoloaders, 162
availability, 162

B

background initialization, creating SANs during, 46
backup controllers, 2
bandwidth
  calculating availability, 26
  calculating need, 24-25
  glossary overview, 162
  metadata network requirements, 14
blocks
  glossary overview, 163
  RAID striping and, 23
Bonjour IP addresses, 42
boot commands, entering Xserve firmware, 51

C

cabling, Fibre Channel
  copper, 87
  optical, 88
cache, 163
cascade loop topology, 85
cascade topology, 84
cascading, 163
centralized directories
  binding client to, 76
  building SAN with, 67
  determining permissions with, 63
  setting up groups, 73
  setting up primary groups, 75

setting up users, 75
client computers
  memory requirements, 7
  RAID Admin connection to, 42
  as Xsan SAN component, 2
  in Xsan topology examples, 17, 19, 22
client set up, 67-79
  binding client to directory, 76
  building SAN with centralized directories, 67
  changing Home folder ownership, 72
  checking for successful client binding, 79
  creating directory entry, 77-78
  G5 PCI slot configuration, 68
  permissions with local authentication, 69
  setting up groups (centralized directory), 73
  setting up primary groups (centralized directory), 75
  setting up users (centralized directory), 74
  User ID setup, 70
  viewing and changing UID and group ID, 71
  in Xsan Admin configuration, 111
clients
  adding, 109
  glossary overview, 164
  Macintosh clients added to StorNext SAN, 128-129
  overview of, 3
  StorNext clients, controllers used with, 128-129
  version information (cvversions), 149
cluster files systems, 164
command line
  cvadmin, 134-135
  cvaffinity, 142
  cvcp, 143
  cvdb, 143
  cvdbset, 143
  cvfsck, 144
  cvfsd, 144
  cvgather, 145-146
  cvlabel, 146
  cvmkdir, 147

174

N

O

P

Index

X

Xsan
    clients, 3
    defining, 1
    metadata controllers, 3
    SAN (storage area network), 2
    SAN volumes, 3
    steps in running, 107
    topologies. *see* topologies, Xsan
Xsan Admin
    listing duplicate LUNs, 153
    LUNs not listed in after slicing, 155
    Storage tab, 119
    unable to connect to SAN computer
        from, 156
XSAN Tuner application, 126
Xserve
    configuring Xsan with, 5
    RAID. *see* RAID (redundant array of
        independent disks)
Xserve G5 servers, 50

Z

zoning, 171

182